WHAT READERS HAVE SAID ABOUT THIS BOOK:

"Effective techniques for positive mental magic written in a readily understandable style."

S.F. in Circle Network News, Madison, WI

"Your book, *Creative Visualization*, is an absolute gift that I've been waiting for!"

Noel F., Toluca Lake, CA

"This is another practical guide of progressive exercises for "Magickal Power and Spiritual Attainment.' I would recommend this book for people who are looking to begin meditation and guided imagery. There is no documentation and this is not a study guide, but simply a book of practical exercises to develop your psychic abilities."

Diana M. Peake in SSC Booknews, Rockville, MD

" . . . I am writing to inquire of you about getting additional copies of CREATIVE VISUALIZATION. This book has become practically my Bible and my friends over here are tremendously impressed with it and would also like to have their own copies. . . . I have read umpteen 'self-help' books over the years and believe me, as I am sure you know, your's certainly is the most concise, thorough, and 'helpful' of the lot. I can't think of a better gift to give friends I care for."

Brend P., Tonbridge, Kent, England

"Quite ordinary people do seem to perform supernormal feats now and then. Is such power a real possibility? If so, how can we learn to unearth and control it? All things you will ever want or need must have their beginnings in your mind. CREATIVE VISUALIZATION can help you to realize your deepest desires and achieve your greatest potential. Are you yearning for wealth, success, happiness, or spiritual satisfaction? Do you know how to use your powers to get what you want—or do you misuse them unknowingly and fail? This easy series of step-by-step exercises can change your life!"

Kay Sexton in Hooked on Books, Minneapolis, MN

" . . . very exciting, and plainly written. Also it is easy to understand and down to earth."

Sulieman Y., Philadelphia, PA

"Anyone buying the book because they are attracted by the advertising will find that they are learning much more than 'how to get things' as the book's ethical stand is to advocate a 'way of life' in accordance with spiritual laws. . . . it is a gentle way of introducing people to the use of magic.

"The authors of the Guide are the British adepts responsible for the series *Magical Philosophy* and as with its predecessor, the *Practical Guide to Astral Projection* this work is firmly grounded in the theory of *Magical Philosophy*. The book can be worked with at many levels and its techniques are effective. (As its reviewer I personally 'tested' some of the techniques and had excellent results. I also received glowing reports from some friends who had acquired the book in the last few months and were working with it.)

"The format of a manual is again followed and in the frontpiece the authors invite readers to write to them about their success (or problems) with the methods they have given in the book. It is a nice touch—so often writers publishing techniques seem unwilling to dialogue with the readers who try them out. Highly recommended for the beginner and the more advanced student."

Ma Deva Gitika in Aquarian Arrow, London, England

"I received first prize in the drawing we had last night. I am sure reading some parts of your book has had influences in the success I experienced in creative visualization . . . "

D.W., Hillsboro, OR

"I already have the Astral Projection, Psychic Self-Defense, and Creative Visualization books, and am very pleased with them. I have really begun to tap my latent psychic talents."

David S., Lisle, IL

"This book is a good basic manual for neophytes beginning to study the applications of visualizations and imagination in Wicca and Magick. It would also come in handy to a solitary practitioner who can not find a good teacher or guide. Explanations are clear and precise, and exercises are detailed and laid out well. It can even throw some light on the various approaches and the 'whys' of certain practices for the more advanced practitioner of magick. When it comes right down to it *Creative Visualization* is a handy little volume to acquire if you're a beginner, and one worth browsing through it you are a little further along."

Lord Elrond in Moonstone, Chamblee, GA

IT'S TRUE...

YOU CAN HAVE WHATEVER YOU WANT!

E=MC^2

Energy and Matter are one and the same thing - the POWER OF THE ATOM and the PLENTY OF THE UNIVERSE are yours *by Divine Right!*

Once you know and employ the principles of Creative Visualization (and the secret methods withheld until now) NO ONE CAN PREVENT YOU FROM ATTAINING YOUR GOALS - WHETHER FOR MATERIAL WEALTH, PROFESSIONAL SUCCESS, HEALTH AND PERSONAL HAPPINESS, OR SPIRITUAL DEVELOPMENT.

NO ONE BUT YOU!

Only you can LIBERATE THE POWER and FOCUS IT TO TRANSFORM YOUR LIFE!

With this book in your hands, you can - if you study and apply these principles - have whatever you want!

About the Authors

Melita Denning and Osborne Phillips are among the most popular authors who are advancing magical knowledge and technique in today's world. They are amply qualified to write with authority on these subjects by their extensive practical experience in magick, and by their long membership in the Qabalistic Order Aurum Solis—totaling nearly fifty years between them. In addition, the high grades of initiation they both hold in the Western Mystery Tradition give them insight into the needs of the student and a vision of the potential of Humanity in this age—making their books a treasury of guidance and teaching of paramount importance.

Melita Denning is the first woman Grand Master of Aurum Solis, a position she has held since 1976. She was invested Dame d'Honneur, O.M.C.T., in 1968, by the Geneva Grand Priory of the Sovereign Military Order of the Temple.

Osborne Phillips is currently Administrator-General of Aurum Solis. He is a Fellow of the International Biographical Association, a Life Patron of the American Biographical Institute and member of the Institute's National Advisory Board, and an Honorary Fellow of the Anglo-American Academy.

Both are listed in various editions of *International Authors and Writers Who's Who, Who's Who in the World, Contemporary Authors, Dictionary of International Biography* and *Personalities of West and Midwest.* Melita Denning is also listed in *Directory of Distinguished Americans, World Who's Who of Women* and *International Who's Who in Community Service.* Osborne Phillips is also listed in *Men of Achievement* and *Men and Women of Distinction.*

To Write to the Authors

We cannot guarantee that every letter written to the authors can be answered, but all will be forwarded to them. Both the authors and the publisher appreciate hearing from readers, learning of your enjoyment and benefit from this book. Llewellyn also publishes a bi-monthly news magazine with news and reviews of practical esoteric studies and articles helpful to the student, and some readers' questions and comments to the authors may be answered through this magazine's columns if permission to do is included in the original letter. The authors and their advanced students sometimes participate in seminars and workshops, and dates and places are announced in *The Llewellyn New Times.* To write to the authors, or to ask a question, write to:

Denning and Phillips
c/o THE LLEWELLYN NEW TIMES
P.O. Box 64383, Dept. 183, St. Paul, MN 55164-0383, U.S.A.
Please enclose a self-addressed, stamped envelope for reply, or $1.00 to cover costs.

About the Llewellyn Practical Guides
to Personal Power

To some people, the idea the "Magick" is *practical* comes as a surprise. It shouldn't!

The entire basis for what we call "Magick" is to exercise influence over one's personal world in order to satisfy our needs and goals. And, while this Magick is also concerned with Psychological Transformation and Spiritual Growth, even the spiritual life must be built on firm material foundations.

> **PRACTICAL: available, useable, and valuable in actions applied to useful purposes, contributing toward a better life.**

That's what we mean. Here are techiniques that will help you to a better life, will help you attain things you want, will help you in your personal growth and development. *Moreover, these books can change your life, dynamically, positively!*

> **Success, Attainment, Happiness. Miracles! Powers of ESP, Healing, out-of-body travel! Clairvoynace and Divination! Extended Powers of Mind and Body! Communication with non-physical beings, Knowledge by non-material means!**

We've always known of things like this . . . seemingly super-normal achievements, often by quite ordinary people. We are told that we normally use only 10% of our Human Potential. We are taught that Faith can move mountains, that Love heals all hurt, that Miracles do occur. We believe these things to be true, but most people lack practical knowledge of them.

The material world and the psychic are intertwined, and it is this that establishes the Magickal Link: that Mind/Soul/Spirit can as easily influence the material as vice versa.

"Psychic Powers" and Magickal Practices can, and should, be used in one's daily life. Each of us has many wonderful, but yet under-developed talents and powers—surely we have an evolutionary obligation to make full use of our Human Potentials! Mind and Body work together, and Magick is simply the extension of this interaction into dimensions beyond the limits normally conceived. *Why be limited?*

All things you will ever want or be must have their start in your mind. In these books you are given practical guidance to develop your inner powers and apply them to your everyday needs. These abilities will eventually belong to everybody through natural evolution, but you can learn and develop them now!

For other books in this series, please refer to the back pages of this book. Those that are already published, and those that are forthcoming, form a full library of Magickal knowledge and practice.

OTHER BOOKS FROM THE AUTHORS

The Magical Philosophy*—A Study of the Western Mystery Tradition
  Book I, *Robe and Ring*, 1974
  Book II, *The Apparel of High Magick*, 1975
  Book III, *The Sword and the Serpent*, 1975
  Book IV, *The Triumph of Light*, 1978
  Book V, *Mysteria Magica*, 1982

The Llewellyn Practical Guide(s) to:
  Astral Projection, 1979
  Psychic Self-Defense & Well-Being, 1980
  The Development of Psychic Powers, 1981
  The Magick of Sex, 1982
  The Magick of the Tarot, 1983

The Llewellyn New Age Series:
  The Inner World of Fitness (by Melita Denning)

The Llewellyn Mystery Religion Series:
  Voudoun Fire: The Living Reality of Mystical Religion

The Llewellyn Deep Mind Tape(s) for:
  Astral Projection and the Out-of-Body Experience, 1981

The Llewellyn Inner Guide(s) to:
  Magical States of Consciousness, 1985

The Llewellyn Inner Guide Tape(s):
  Paths to Inner Worlds, Series I (tapes—Paths 32 to 24), 1985

Other Books and Tapes Forthcoming:
  The Llewellyn Inner Guide to Planetary Magick
  The Llewellyn Practical Guide to Talismanic Magick
  The Magical Philosophy, Revised, in Three Volumes
  Fire Out of Eden
  Evocation of the Gods
  Moving with Power
  The World of Celtic Magic

Also forthcoming:
  A Correspondence Course in the Western Esoteric Tradition

For current information on books & tapes and other activities of the authors, and regarding the Order Aurum Solis, see *The Llewellyn New Times* bi-monthly news magazine and catalog from:
LLEWELLYN PUBLICATIONS
P.O. Box 64383-183
St. Paul, MN 55164-0383, U.S.A

the Llewellyn Practical Guide to

Creative
Visualization

**The Dynamic Way to
Success, Love, Plenty
and Spiritual Power**

Second Edition, Revised and Enlarged, 1983

Melita Denning &
Osborne Phillips

1988
LLEWELLYN PUBLICATIONS
St. Paul, Minnesota, 55164-0383, U.S.A.

International Standard Book Number: 0-87542-183-0
Library of Congress Catalog Number: 83-80168

First Edition, 1980
Second Edition, 1983
Seventh Printing, 1987
Ninth Printing, 1988

Library of Congress Cataloging-in-Publication Data
Denning, Melita.
    The Llewellyn practical guide to creative visualization: the
    dynamic way to success, love, plenty and spiritual power.
    Melita Denning & Osborne Phillips. — 2nd ed.   rev. and
    enl. — St. Paul, Minn., U.S.A.: Llewellyn Publications, 1983.

    xxi. 250 p., ill., 21 cm.
    1. Success.   2. Imagery (Psychology).   3. Visualization.

    I. Phillips, Osborne.   II. Title.   III. Title: Creative visual-
    ization.
    BF637.S8D373   1983   131—dc19   83-80168
    ISBN 0-87542-183-0

Produced by Llewellyn Publications
Typography and Art property of Chester-Kent, Inc.

Published by
LLEWELLYN PUBLICATIONS
A Division of Chester-Kent, Inc.
P.O. Box 64383
St. Paul, MN 55164-0383, U.S.A.

Printed in the United States of America

Contents

1 Control and Direct Your Personal Destiny
People visualize whether they know it or not. Visualization is creative. Visualizing for what you want. Getting all levels of yourself to co-operate. The Eastern mystic and the cave-man: image, action, chant. A vivid imagination? Link it to reality! When to talk, when to be silent. How to make a start. Daydreams can help: think of what you want most in the world! "Seeing" a remembered image. Useful aids. You visualize with your mind, not with your eyes.   1

2 The Potent Circle
Tension is a natural prelude to action. Unresolved tension is the enemy, so cultivate relaxation for inner progress and bodily health. A Yogi's secret. The Creative Plan of Relaxation: full directions. Your real self is pure

joy! The "Potent Circle": greater bodily awareness and relaxation brings more effective well-wishing to each part, which brings greater bodily awareness and relaxation. Rhythmic Breath, the necessary accompaniment to Creative Relaxation.   27

3 **You Have A Great Future!**
Organizing your Creative Visualization practices. Getting maximum help from the sub-rational levels of the psyche but not letting them take control. The Higher Self, which should control and direct the Rational Mind. Our need to realize we are an integral part of the universe. Plan joyfully for your future, and sing about it!   51

4 **The Life-Sustaining Flow**
The true source of plenty needs to be understood for successful Creative Visualization. The four levels of human existence and of the external universe: divine, mental, astral, material. Interaction of the levels. Creating a channel for divine power. Transience of changes caused by astral means only. Don't inhibit your invocation of higher powers by hidden guilt feelings! Ethics of Creative Visualization. New Testament teachings. The meaning of money. The Higher Self. Bringing through power and charging yourself with it.   67

5 **Spiritual Abundance**
Work with your one spiritual source of supply, not with the many possible material ones. The objective you

visualize for is at once yours: astrally, mentally, spiritually. The material realization is to come! Why you are warned not to visualize a material source of supply. Other mistakes to avoid. Be frequently aware of the existence of your spiritual source of supply! Song dispels fear.   93

6 **The Stairway of Success**
"Nothing succeeds like success." Don't attempt to try to explain your secret: just manifest what it does for you! Other people's imaginations will help you to further successes *so long as those people can identify with you*. The Charging Technique and the Master Method: their use in Creative Visualization to help yourself and others. Working "divination in reverse" with the Charging Technique.   115

7 **Star-Points and Multiplication**
Minor techniques of Creative Visualization are less sure than the full Master Method because they are less complete, but they are still very powerful. Their special value while you still need practice in the Foundation Work. Benefits of the Star Technique include bringing opportunities. The Star Technique and how to use it. What happens if you already have some of what you need but it is in any way inadequate? The "secret" examined. The Multiplication Technique.   147

8 Dare to Be Powerful!
Creative Visualization for objectives you may not find it simple to visualize. Build for outer assets and inner development in balanced measure to enjoy the best of both! Special values of Creative Relaxation. Program to break a habit: how to stop smoking as an example. Creative Visualization for better memory: speeches, drama, facts. Memorizing words vs. memorizing meanings. General absent-mindedness. What is a gizmo? Family birthdays—elementary astrology can turn "words" into "meanings." 169

Appendices

A Terminating a Creative Visualization Process
Usually when one objective in Creative Visualization has been sufficiently attained and the conscious mind resolves upon the next objective, the emotional-instinctual nature will follow its lead. Why this may not always be so. Technique to terminate effectively a Creative Visualization process if necessary. Use of this technique to stop the visualization of an image created involuntarily. 197

B Helping Others See Your Vision
You need to be able to help other people see your vision and act on it. Teachers, preachers, politicians, attorneys, lecturers and the many others to whom this

ability is vital must begin by making themselves as positive and dynamic as possible, with Creative Relaxation.
Don't "stand in the way of" the picture you want to
create! People close the doors of their rational mind;
they can't close the doors of their emotional-instinctual
nature. The way to win a fair hearing. Ethics of persuasion. How non-ethical persuasion breaks down.
What to visualize and how to talk about it.   205

C The Bright Lamp of Knowledge
Wisdom Texts to aid your Creative Visualization
learning and motivation.   219

D Creative Visualization in Prayer and Worship
Creative Visualization comes more easily to followers
of a religion with established images. How to develop
your personal prayer and worship rituals. The relationship
between the Image and the Spirit. The building of your
alter. Steps to development of a prayer ritual. Using an
intermediary being. Maintaining your focus on a particular
deity.   227

E Maintaining Good Health
You can use Creative Visualization to help you
maintain good health. Creative Visualization and weight
control. Creative Visualization can help you achieve
deep, restful sleep. The Deep Mind is a powerful instrument
which needs to be controlled by the directive, rational
mind. Breathing correctly is essential.   237

"Study Points" are part of the unique approach used in the Llewellyn Practical Guides series of books dealing with the 'technology' of Magick and the seemingly super-normal powers of the Deep Mind: "Study Points" outline certain concepts important to the chapter that follows—not as an outline of the contents, but as points which are emphasized by calling them to your attention in advance of the context in which they will appear.

Each chapter is followed by a "Check Point" which serves as re-inforcement of certain of the concepts, and of the practices, that have been presented. The "Check Point" is more than a review; it is a reiteration of the steps taken in the steady and progressive development in this practical and modern method of training the hidden faculties of mind and psyche.

Introduction

CREATIVE VISUALIZATION!

What is it?

Before answering the question, let me assure you
that it is not difficult to do (in fact, everyone does
it—but most people do it "negatively" with results that
are bad for them). The difficult part was done long ago
—in evolving the amazing complex and powerful being
that we call human.

We talk about "the efficient use of our natural
resources," but we barely tap the potential of our own
selves—*we are the most under-utilized resource imaginable!* We have this wonderful computer we call our
brain; and beyond that we have Consciousness itself.
And we are an organic part of the Universe that is infinite. We have so much that it is actually misleading to say
"we use only 10% of our potential!" The truth is that

we don't even do that. . . . perhaps 10% would be the standard for the average *successful* person in today's world, but the vast majority use far less than that. That's why the vast majority *are not successful!*

What do we mean by "success"? Not just being rich, or having all that you can desire. We mean living a full and meaningful life in which we actually accomplish whatever we set out to do—in being healthy, happy, secure; in our marriage, our finances, our education; in painting a picture or building a bridge; in top level performance on the job and in getting the job we want; in becoming the person we want to be.

What is Creative Visualization? We can call it "Success Power." It means to have an idea, or an *image*, of what we want to *create:* recognizing that to fulfull our goals (no matter what they may be) we have to imagine our present reality transformed into something that we want—and then to accomplish that *transformation!*

We can also say that Creative Visualization is that which sets the human being off from those other life forms for whom success is mostly survival. Also, we can individually manage our own destiny...accepting it as personal responsibility. Living on welfare will never make you rich, nor secure; stealing might give you money, for a while, but it leaves you with increased problems for the next day's needs—just as eating the "seed corn" might fill your stomach today, but leave you without the means to plant for next season's harvest.

But there's more to success than survival! We have many goals—mostly measured, whether in economic or in spiritual terms, by our distance above the survival level. We may desire "things;" we may want to be beautiful and attractive, respected and admired; we may want position, recognition, or security; we look for a lover, mate, child, friend; we seek knowledge, ability, powers. And we may arrange our goals in a series of stepping stones, a stairway from lesser to greater. . . each being a foundation for the next. We can make a plan, or a map, for going from one level of accomplishment to the next. That's sensible—and certainly you must learn to examine your goals and make such a plan.

But there is more to success than accomplishing one goal after another. There's what sometimes has been called "the Luck Factor": the ability to attract the opportunities to make for success. Desire is a form of energy, an "emotional electricity," we might say. And when you feed electricity into something it always creates a magnetic field. But, this can work in two ways.

An American President once said: "The only thing we have to fear is fear itself." Fear attracts the very things we don't want! Fear is a very powerful emotion, and that energy, tied in with an image of the thing feared, creates the very circumstances for the feared thing to happen.

A simple example: you can easily walk on top of a wood plank that's flat on the ground—but place that same plank between two step-ladders, and your image of falling becomes so powerful that you probably will fall. (But, under hypnosis, where the image of falling is replaced with an "illusion" that the plank is still on the floor, you will most likely succeed.)

However, the Luck Factor is more than "creating illusions" for oneself! As contrasted with the techniques for successfully accomplishing specific goals that you will be taught in this book, it is the general positive dynamic (that you will also be taught in this book) we commonly identify with "self-confidence," "poise," "winning," etc. It includes the "positive self-image" in which you see yourself as the kind of person you want to be, living the kind of life you want to live—healthy, wealthy, happy, successful, beautiful, surrounded by friends and *opportunities*. Opportunity does not knock only once! A successful person attracts opportunities—but opportunities are the field in which to plant and nurture, and bring to harvest the specific goals you have. And, amazingly, a powerful Luck Factor will often seem to repel possibilities of injury or failure. It's an AURA or "Force Field" within which a special environment is created.

What makes the difference between one person's success and another's failure? There are well-educated failures—so it's not just a matter of education. There are failures from "good" families as well as "bad," and successes from "the other side of the tracks" as well as the right side—so it's not just a matter of "contacts" or "class." There are people who fail at whatever they do, no matter how much they may be helped by government, nor how many times they have opened their doors to opportunity's knock.

And there are people who finally rise to success, overcoming obstacles and even handicaps, even when they have failed before. And there are other people who are successful in everything they do, who have never suffered a failure of any sort. And sometimes the magnitude of their successs is so great, or the "luck" which surrounds them so amazing, that we thing of them as blessed. These are people who "believe in themselves" and in what they are doing; their vision is often so great that it encompasses a nation, a people, a world.

No matter what else it seems, the essence of SUCCESS POWER is in the techniques of Creative Visualization taught in this book. Recognizing that we all have far greater potentiality than we normally use, we will say that CREATIVE VISUALIZATION IS A TECHNIQUE FOR MOBILIZING OUR INNER RESOURCES FOR SUCCESS.

Inside each of us there is a giant engine, usually just barely idling along; there's a powerful computer, normally just barely operating; there's a great dynamo mostly just producing a fraction of the energy it could;

and there's a "programmer" who can put all this tremendous capacity to work in order to accomplish whatever we want. CREATIVE VISUALIZATION IS A WAY TO GIVE INSTRUCTIONS TO THE PROGRAMMER.

We think in terms of three dimensions, sometimes we talk in terms of four—but we actually live in a Universe of many dimensions, and it is from some of these other dimensions that we can attract the opportunities for success. CREATIVE VISUALIZATION IS A METHOD TO OPEN CHANNELS FROM THESE OTHER DIMENSIONS TO BRING US THE WEALTH OF THE UNIVERSE.

This book does more than "tell you about" wonderful things. . . it does more than tell you that wealth and happiness and success can be yours if only you will "believe" or if you will "think positively." With a series of easy-to-follow exercises, your mind will be programmed to bring your desires into personal realization. You will be able to CHANGE YOUR LIFE!

And we want to share your successes. We want to know how Creative Visualization changes your life, bringing you success and happiness. We invite you to write to us, to the authors in care of the publisher, and tell us what you've done. Sometimes we may want to use your success story as an example for others—for your accomplishment helps set a pattern of accomplishment for others. The success of each person multiplies the opportunities for success for all of us—remember that the Universe itself is infinite, and when we use the techniques of Creative Visualization the wealth we obtain is not a subtraction from that available to someone else, but a total enrichment of this material plane.

CREATIVE VISUALIZATION PUTS THE UNIVERSE TO WORK FOR YOU. And, using the techniques of Creative Visualization puts you into a positive relationship with the dynamics of the Universe. Every creative act brings you into greater harmony with the "Force" behind all that is.

May the Force be with you!

Carl Llewellyn Weschcke
Publisher

Study Points

1

Creative Visualization is a natural power we all possess.

1. Creative Visualization, used with knowledge and awareness, CAN TRANSFORM YOUR LIFE!

2. Most of us do Creative Visualization — all the time — but because we do not do it consciously, effectively and beneficially, it is more often destructive than constructive . . . making "bad luck" instead of "good luck!"

3. Most of this Creative Mind Power is wasted because of conflicts within — unresolved desires and instincts and even unknown fears — that rob us of success.

4. To liberate this natural power to fulfill your desires, *you must bring together all the faculties,*

the senses, the brain itself, into a "unified field," eliminating all "interior" barriers to the attainment of your goals.

a. Unity requires a method that will:
   1. Be controlled by your *Rational Mind.*
   2. Appeal to your *Emotions.*
   3. Be accepted by your *Instincts.*
   4. Enlist the help of your *Physical Senses.*
   (Think of the formula R I P E — Rational Mind, Instincts, Physical Senses, Emotions — you must create the conditions that allow your chosen goals to RIPEN.)

5. The First Requirement is like "daydreaming" and is used to WAKE UP THE EMOTIONAL NATURE.
   a. The First Requirement is to:
      1. Image the desired goal.
      2. Augment the imaged goal with real or imaged physical action, thus *uniting the inner and outer worlds.*
   b. This activity is enhanced by:
      1. Silence — don't dissipate the inner energies by talking about your inner working.
      2. Visualizing things in connection with your goal — seeing things as they will be.
      3. Feeling the emotional satisfaction that will be yours — enjoy it now.

Control and Direct Your Destiny

1

People are strolling about, talking: filling in time at an air terminal, or maybe bringing their family gossip up to date at a reunion. A middle-aged man speaks:

"Bert? Oh, yes, he's doing well; but then, he's always known what he wanted. Following in his father's footsteps, all right — looking more like the old man every day, too!"

A young girl tells her friends, "Of course I'm thrilled, it's right out of this world! But do you know, I could just *see* myself in that part? I said to myself from the beginning, 'That's me, that's me!' It *had* to work out!"

Another man says, "Everything's okay just now, but I'm keeping my fingers crossed. The family's okay, I'm okay, the job's going along fine — but you know my luck. Mark my words, I'm just waiting to see what goes wrong!"

There is nothing very unusual about the stories told in all these speeches. You can hear something along the same lines in any gathering of people. They show a variety of viewpoints, but also they all reveal one very interesting factor. *Consciously or unconsciously, helpfully or harmfully, many people — in fact, most people — perform creative visualization all the time.*

This book will tell you, in detail, how to perform Creative Visualization. But further, it will also teach you how to perform Creative Visualization

CONSCIOUSLY
EFFECTIVELY
BENEFICIALLY

to enrich your life and to reach your own personal objectives.

What you will be learning here is a directed and extremely valuable method of doing something which is in any case one of your natural human abilities. Controlled and directed by your conscious mind, *it can give you A PROGRESSIVE, AND IMMENSE, POWER TO CONTROL AND DIRECT YOUR PERSONAL DESTINY!*

You will also learn how to *avoid* performing Creative Visualization, for instance when you have obtained a sufficient supply of something you needed, or when you have to give thought to something you fear.

KNOWN FROM THE EARLIEST TIMES WHICH HAVE YIELDED EVIDENCE OF HUMAN THOUGHTS, TAUGHT TO BELIEVERS IN ONE RELIGION AFTER ANOTHER, CREATIVE VISUALIZATION IS THE MOST POTENT SINGLE TECHNIQUE OF SELF-FULFILLMENT IN ALL THE RANGE OF HUMAN CAPABILITIES. Its scope ranges from the cave-dweller's simple desire for the meat that was his food, to the sublime yearning of the Eastern mystic to be free from all desire. In both these cases, and in every instance, the answer is the same: know — *see* — that what you seek is yours already, AND IT IS YOURS ALREADY.

There have been instances — at many different levels of need — where realization of that truth was at once total and entire, and no further work upon it was needed. In most cases, however, and for most people, something more is required to bring about the desired fulfillment. *This is not because of some "fate" outside ourselves, not because of some decree in the objective universe;* it is simply because we are such complex creatures. The intellect, the emotions, the unconscious levels of the psyche, the bodily nervous system, all can pull in different directions. Yet in spite of this disunity, most of us feel sure that we want this or that, we need this or that, something of a material kind or something non-material. What is necessary is to bring *all* the faculties of the psyche, plus the bodily senses and the physical brain, into accord for the goal to be achieved.

It may take some time to do this — and when it is done, there may be some inertia or even some opposition in the outer world to be overcome, but overcome IT WILL BE. Drops of water will wear away rock. Delicate growing shoots will push up a heavy paving stone. That which is without purpose must yield to whatever has a living, driving purpose.

How, then, are you to bring, as swiftly and effectively as possible, all the levels of your being into a united and co-ordinated drive for what you want? How devise a method that will —

Be controlled by your *Rational Mind*
Appeal to your *Emotions*
Be accepted by your *Instincts*
Enlist the help of your *Physical Senses*.

There are several such methods, since the physical senses can be brought in by means of *Sounds (Words),* or by *Bodily Action,* for example, both of which will be introduced later in this book. The first, and principal, means of "enlisting the help of the physical senses" is concerned however with the sense of *Sight.*

It is by means of Sight that people have chiefly proceeded in these techniques for obtaining whatever they need, although usually — and wisely — this has been reinforced by other action at the material level. (After all, it is at the material level that you need your desires to be realized, since you are living in this material world here and now. Even if a person had no need to wish for anything save "to go to Heaven when he dies," he is in this world wishing it, and in fact all the religions agree that matters of this kind have to be determined while one *is* living in this world.)

Let us go back, then, to considering our two extreme examples: our Eastern mystic who desires only to desire nothing, and our cave-man who desires meat for his and his family's next meal. Since there is so much difference in what they want, do we find a similar great difference in their ways of setting about it?

Not at all! Both are human beings, intent on the fulfillment (at different levels and in different circumstances) of their human nature. Of course the details differ, but *the basic methods are the same.* The Eastern mystic has his Buddha-rupa, or something similar: an image or symbol of the ideal he is pursuing. He sits meditatively before this, using his sight to imprint the symbol in his brain-cells and in his mind; if there is an image (as a Buddha-rupa) he will sit in a posture similar to that of the image. We know that he uses certain chants, "mantrams," to lead his mind in the same way by means of the sense of hearing.

Our cave-man, on the other hand, drew pictures with great skill and accuracy of the animals he wished to hunt down. Some of these, perhaps, were simply looked at. Evidence shown that spears — real spears, model spears, or in some cases just the paintings of spears — were hurled, or were added to the pictures as if they had been hurled, so that *the appropriate physical action* was brought into the procedure. Whether the cave-men chanted, made suitable sounds, we naturally cannot say on evidence; but by comparison with the actions of some people in Africa and other regions in modern times it is very likely. There is also among the cave-paintings of France a very famous, unique and precious Magician-figure, wearing an animal-mask and apparently dancing; there again we have physical mimicry and special actions, only now performed by one individual, probably for the benefit of a whole community.

Why have these creative actions — the image, the action, the chant — been employed by people in different lands, of different cultures, and for widely different purposes, over and over through thousands of years?

BECAUSE THEY WORK. THEY BRING THE DESIRED RESULT, ALIGNING EVERY LEVEL OF THE INDIVIDUAL WITH THE DESIRE SO THAT THERE IS NO BARRIER TO ITS ATTAINMENT.

AND WHEN THERE IS NO BARRIER TO WHAT WE WANT, WE MEET WITH IT AS SURELY AS THE MAGNET MEETS WITH IRON!

That is true whether what we want is an inward power, or a skill, or a material object, or a piece of information, or a person to help us in an enterprise or to accompany us in life; or all these things at different times.

A vivid imagination, the ability to "daydream," can and certainly should be turned to good account; but a temperament with these characteristics is not at all necessary for success, and is by itself no guarantee of effective Creative Visualization. *The "know-how" is essential.* Some people do have it naturally, or come by it intuitively: but NOT ALL VISUALIZATION IS CREATIVE, and if we do not find, or learn, the means *to link the inner and outer levels* in what we are trying to do, the most vivid imagination will not benefit us in any way.

Thomas Chatterton, who lived in England in the eighteenth century, had from childhood a keen mind, with a teeming imagination. He created for himself a dream world of historical and imaginary characters, and in relation to this he produced a volume of beautiful and remarkable poetry. He began contributing prose pieces to various magazines, and when he was seventeen left his home in Bristol for London. Horace Walpole, a notable politician and writer, said of him subsequently, "I do not believe there ever existed so masterly a genius." Apart from his "olde-worlde" style of poetry, he became known as a perceptive and trenchant satirist on the current affairs of his own times. Yet the plain fact is that he was unable, whether by letter or face to face, to obtain even the bare necessities of life.

Chatterton died, starving, before he was eighteen, and the literary world was shocked. Doubtless this tragedy can be attributed to various outer-world causes:

the payment for one piece of his work was delayed after publication, another piece was held over to be published later, a poem was rejected because of its peculiar imitation-antique language. None of these mischances was in itself particularly unusual, or particularly grave; but to Chatterton they all happened at once, and persistently, and he lacked the resources to ride out the storm.

Looking to the inner causes of things, however, we can see that by the pseudo-historical fancies of his poetical writing, as well as by the satirical brilliance of his prose, Chatterton had employed his great imagination, not to unite himself with the world around him, but to separate himself from it. His chosen models and heroes either had a solid family behind them, or were men to whom writing was only a side-line, so they could afford to stand alone in their ideas. This does not mean you should avoid originality, or put aside your convictions. It means you should keep your imagination linked to *reality*: SPIRITUAL REALITY, RATIONAL REALITY, EMOTIONAL REALITY, MATERIAL REALITY. It also means you should PLAN FOR BALANCE in what you decide to visualize; and we shall come back to that later.

VISUALIZE
IN A CONSCIOUS AND
CONTROLLED MANNER, AND YOU ARE
BUILDING FOR SUCCESS.

As with many other kinds of practice with your inner faculties, it is not generally desirable to let other people know more than that you are "interested in" these matters. (Of course you should only tell them even that much if you feel sure they are sympathetic; and in any case, do assume that at some time they'll tell others.) Apart from the detriment that could occur to your inner work from the things other people say to you, especially in the early stages of your development, or *even from things they think* — YOU are working mostly by thought, aren't you? — there is the danger of de-fusing your own activity by the mere act of talking about it.

If you are excited, perplexed or disturbed about anything, frequently the quickest way to an easier state of mind is to talk about it. This may or may not help in the long run, depending largely on the character of the person you talk to, but at least for the time it dissipates your pattern of thought and emotion. So take care with the Creative Visualization thoughts and images *which you don't want dissipated:* guard them from contact AS YOU WOULD GUARD THE GROWING TIP OF A TREASURED PLANT!

All the same, it is sometimes only the *inner* action that need be hidden; the outer work may then be plain for all to see, and if people think about it at all they may think they understand the whole operation. What does that matter, so long as the desired result is creditably achieved?

As an example: A young man was working in a machine-shop, shaping small engine-parts on the various millers, routers and other machines. His immediate ambition was to get on to the big capstan-lathes, a job which carried more prestige as well as more money than what he was doing, and which was coveted by a number of other lads besides himself.

This young man was not content, however, merely to wish. His mother knew something of the work of the mind, and although hitherto he had paid little heed to her hints on the subject, he recalled something valuable now. He watched the skilled men working on the capstans, noting even their stance and the movements they performed; and often at lunch-breaks he took a quick look at the machines themselves, the way they were set up, their cutters and the work they did. *But this was not all.*

He took great care to go on doing his present work efficiently, but *at every time of relaxation* (this was the "secret" part of his operation) *he closed his eyes for a few moments and PICTURED himself working on one of the capstans, confidently going through the motions he had seen, swiftly and skillfully moving, turning and co-ordinating the wheels and levers which controlled the heavy machine. He saw gleaming and perfectly shaped piston-heads and other parts coming from under the cutter.*

After a few weeks, it happened that by a quite normal sequence of events a chance came for someone to be put temporarily on the capstans: an opportunity to learn, and to become recognized as a future capstan operator. Our young man volunteered, and secured the job. Later the foreman said to him, "What really decided it was your confidence in taking the controls. You will do well, *and I'm really not surprised.* I've seen you, many a time, looking the old capstans over!"

This is more complex. A girl wanted to live in a distant country, but could see no prospect of getting there. As it meant a lot to her, she studied the language, and began Creative Visualization, with the "Star" technique (given in Chapter 7). Then she was offered a vacation in another land, much nearer home than the one she wanted. She accepted: it was a beginning.

On that vacation she exchanged addresses with several people. Most of these acquaintanceships faded out; however, she kept up her "Star" practice, and the next year, quite unexpectedly, one of these contacts, an older woman, wrote again. She had come into some money and wanted to travel further, but would not dare go alone. Remembering, however, how much our friend enjoyed travel, she ventured to invite her . . .

So they set out; but events took another turn. An outbreak of hostilities forced the older woman to curtail her plan. She returned home—but the girl did not; she remained, doing welfare work, in the very land of her dreams! *Had her wish been fulfilled the year before, she would have had no way to remain there.*

One of the interesting things about visualization is that it is good for you to be able to visualize so many things in connection with it. It is not only your goal that you should visualize: the clearer your idea of what you are doing, the better you will be able to do it. To begin with, here is an experiment which will tell you something useful:

Try now to visualize, or at least to hold in mind, some good-sized landmark: one you see fairly often, or one you know from pictures. It could be your City Hall, or the Taj Mahal, or the Leaning Tower of Pisa, or perhaps a mountain. Let it be something whose general outline you can easily think of, even if at this stage you can't mentally "see" it. (If you want to refresh your memory before trying, a picture is often clearer for this purpose than the real thing.) Close your eyes and "see" it as clearly as you can; if at the present stage you can't achieve this, you still probably will be able mentally to "work around the outline." Either way, make it so that it seems to be about the size of a matchbox.

When you have the outline as steady as you can make it, *or at least a distinct "feeling" of the object being visually present to you,* it may seem to be in front of your eyes or it may seem to be floating somewhere inside your head. Never mind where it seems to be at this stage! *Still keeping your eyes closed,* raise a finger and, bringing it towards yourself, *try to touch the middle of your mental picture.* Do it so that if you were viewing your picture through a little daylight viewer, your finger-tip would make a dark blob in the middle of the scene.

You feel your finger-tip make contact with your forehead — where? *Most likely it is in the area just above and between your eyebrows.*

Repeat the experiment, make sure of the spot, and *press your finger-tip there quite hard for about thirty seconds,* so that you are still conscious of that exact spot after you have taken your finger away.

Now you have just made an important discovery. When you practice visualization in the various ways you will find in this book, you will find it much easier, more convincing to yourself and more effective, if you know from the beginning *where you are "putting" the picture.* Repeat this experiment, with the finger pressure, from time to time — say twice a day for a week, then once a day for another week, then just whenever you feel like doing it. *This is not meant to be a burdensome "exercise;" it is just an informal and easy practice which will help a great deal with your visualization.*

Notice other people: how often, when they are trying to remember something, or to do a mental calculation, or to deal with anything that may need to be visualized, how often the fingers go naturally to that region of the forehead!

It is true that the ability to visualize is not the same in everyone. It is not always the same even in one person at different ages, or in different states of health. Many people who, as youngsters, are gifted with a faculty of very vivid visualization, find that they lose this faculty to a greater or less degree as they grow older. Women often seem to keep this faculty better than men do, and men whose occupation is not primarily concerned with words or figures (a wide classification including such diverse types as surgeons, farmers, truck-drivers, athletes and artists) seem to keep it better than those whose work leads them to take a more abstract view of life, such as accountants and computer programmers.

IN BETWEEN THESE TWO CLASSIFICATIONS OF MEN THERE IS ANOTHER, WHICH IS A REAL DANGER AREA AS FAR AS VISUALIZATION IS CONCERNED: THE THEORETICAL SIDE OF THEIR WORK, THE PAPERWORK, TENDS TO DEPRIVE THEM OF THIS FACULTY, AND YET THEY VITAL-LY NEED VISUALIZATION — *CREATIVE* VISUAL-IZATION — TO WIN SUCCESS IN THEIR PARTICU-LAR CALLINGS. In this category we have again a wide diversity: lawyers, clergy, teachers, salesmen, all who need to present their message to others in a special way.

This book is planned to make Creative Visualization accessible to everyone: *the particular needs of people with this type of difficulty will be taken into account, as well as the needs of other groups of people. The general plan, however, is for* all alike.

Some people seem unable to visualize *clearly*; others seem unable to control *what* they visualize, or to produce any mental images at all. These difficulties may, certainly, in some cases be due to physical (for instance, glandular) causes, or to a fixed stamp of temperament; but in far more cases they are due only to *habits of mind* which are detrimental to the personality as a whole. These can, and should, be changed.

Habits of mind are not like habits involving physical things, which can be in one way or another addictive. *Habits of mind are dependent entirely upon the emotional nature, and will change precisely as soon as the emotional nature no longer supports them but moves in a different direction.*

And the emotional nature WILL move in a different direction, *as soon as it prefers a contrary object of desire.* But it — the emotional nature — must PREFER the new object. It is not enough that the rational mind sees reason why the new object should be preferable. It is not enough if the new object is preferable by some spiritual law. *The emotional nature must prefer it, see it as its own immediate and most desirable good.* Then it will move every material and non-material obstacle to gain that object, that good.

This is not just true for a few; *it is basic human nature.* It can be a great weakness (for in fact the rational mind cannot long hold us to what the emotional nature does not want) but it can also be our main strength, *when we make the emotional nature work FOR US.*

The emotional nature, in fact, is rather like a small child, who may grasp a sharp knife or some other dangerous thing, not understanding the danger, but just because the object is bright and shiny. What should you do in such a case? *Not* try to take the knife away by force; that could lead to all kinds of trouble! Usually the best thing to do is to take the child's free hand, and then offer to the hand holding the knife something even more attractive, a brightly-colored toy for instance, or something good to eat. If the new object is well chosen and well presented, the knife will soon be dropped.

No matter how mature we may be, in each one of us there is hiding a very juvenile emotional nature! We may be no longer interested in knives and candies, *but when the right objects are found, the same principles apply.*

To succeed in simple visualization (a necessary preliminary to the creative kind) three qualities are chiefly necessary:

RESOLUTION

CONCENTRATION

PATIENCE

These are very often the qualities which, people complain, they find "failing" as they grow older, although this is usually a very mistaken idea. There are (most unfortunately) a lot of people just out of high school who are already showing markedly less of these same qualities than they had, while also there are other people going on through their eighties without any problems of that kind. (Indeed, ELASTICITY OF MIND is one of the best recipes for a long and happy life that the human race has yet discovered.)

Usually the "failing mental powers" of which people complain are nothing more or less than *an unconscious reluctance to put as much effort into cultivating those faculties, as they would cheerfully have given in childhood. There is a submerged feeling that certain efforts have been made, once and for a lifetime, to learn, to acquire skills, to imprint on the brain a number of techniques connected with daily living.*

However, when once the emotional nature TRULY GRASPS the fulfilling, inspiring, LIFE-GIVING purpose of the new enterprise, the VITAL INTEREST AND GREAT ADVANTAGE of gaining or regaining these basic mental skills, then the unconscious objections, the timidity, the inertia, will be gone.

Think of *what you want most in the world.* With the power to visualize rightly controlled and directed, *THAT* CAN BE YOURS!

If you have any difficulties in visualization, now, besides the forehead-touching practice you have been given, THINK MUCH ABOUT WHAT YOU WANT IN LIFE. Never mind whether you can see any possible way to obtain your objectives or not. Whether they are material things or non-material ones, REFLECT ON THEM: picture them to the best of your ability, but above all FEEL IN IMAGINATION THE SENSATION OF POSSESSING THEM, OF DOING WHAT YOU WISH TO DO WITH THEM. If it is a car that you want, imagine driving it; imagine, as clearly as you can, the pleasures and advantages of the particular *kind* of car you want. If it is a person, think of what you would say to such a person, what you would do in the company of such a person. If it is a sum of money, think about what you want it for.

All this is, at the present stage, day-dreaming pure and simple, but it is day-dreaming with a purpose. You are WAKING UP your emotional nature, its unconscious levels included, TO AN AWARENESS OF HOW MUCH YOU WANT THESE THINGS — how much IT wants these things. Get as much *sensation,* and as much *image,* into this day-dreaming as you possibly can — those are languages that the unconscious levels of the psyche understand. If you can't at this stage visualize images, GO AND LOOK AT THE REAL THING, or GET A PICTURE TO REPRESENT IT.

Remember our cave-man and our Eastern mystic. Pictures, images, can be had to represent pretty well anything that a human being might conceivably desire.

Maybe you acutely want several things and there doesn't seem to be any practical connection between them? Never mind that; if you want them all equally,

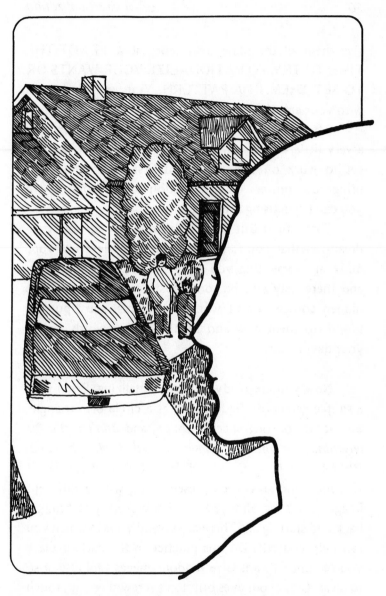

Think of what you want most in the world!

give them all the same treatment; NOW IS NOT THE TIME TO TRY TO RATIONALIZE YOUR WANTS OR TO SET THEM IN A PATTERN. Your concern here is with your emotions, not with your reason.

After a little of this practice — perhaps after only a very little — you will feel that you REALLY want to get to work on this; you want first and foremost to bring your powers of visualization to the point where you can begin using them creatively.

That's fine! But don't altogether give up your day-dreams at that point. The "unconscious" levels of your mind are something you truly are unconscious about, and there may still be some dust to sweep out of the hidden corners. Don't worry about this — just put the broom to them now and then! In other words, re-live your daydreams.

Now you are ready to begin visualizing. Begin with a simple geometric figure, such as a circle or a triangle; but decide on one specific shape, and *don't settle for anything else until you have succeeded with that one.* RESOLUTION — CONCENTRATION — PATIENCE! If your mind strays, or presents you with a different image, *don't* be annoyed or discouraged; just bring it back and start again. There are several ways in which you can help yourself. Do this practice in the darkest place you reasonably can. Give random images a minute or so to clear. Close your eyes but don't screw them up; touch the "visualization point" on your forehead; then if you like you can cup your hands *gently* over your eyes, but take care not to cause any pressure at all on the eyeballs.

When you succeed with this first figure, *keep it there;* don't let it change into something else until you mean it to change! Then decide what you will have next, and make it change promptly, say from a circle to a triangle, or from a triangle to a star. If you want to proceed to somewhat more complex forms the images on standard ESP cards, or a simplified set of Signs of the Zodiac, should give as much practice as anyone would need.

If you persistently have problems with closed eyes, try these other methods too. One is to have a plain black surface of at least twelve inches square, and to try to see the visualized shape in white upon it, as if drawn in chalk. Your eyes, of course, are open for this. Another method which helps some people is to look at an ordinary scene in broad daylight — the view from your window, or even a room full of furniture — and suddenly to "see" your star or circle or whatever it may be, against that background. Such an image often only lasts for a flash, but it can very effectively make you realize the true "inwardness" of visualization. *Visualization is not an optical trick.* As soon as you have done this, if you "cup" your eyes or look at your black surface, you should be able to repeat it.

VISUALIZATION IS SOMETHING YOU DO WITH YOUR MIND, *NOT* SOMETHING YOU DO WITH YOUR EYES.

Remember that your "visualization point" is *between and above* your physical eyes, not identical with them. Visualization, like other skills, involves a "knack" which is acquired with persistent practice but is not easy to put into words. While you are still trying for it, do bear in mind that the image which you visualize *will be there because you put it there;* it will not appear spontaneously, like a ghost. Before you succeed, you will practice best by recalling that it is *not* done by physical sight, and *not* by using the eyes; afterwards, you will visualize quite easily and naturally, just as if you were in fact using your physical eyes!

More help will be given in the next chapter: advice which is meant not only to assist you while learning, but to make ALL your subsequent adventures in visualization better organized, more pleasurable, and for these reasons *more constantly effective.*

Checkpoint

1

- Begin by finding the center-forehead point where your visualized image is to be formed.

- Practice memorizing and visualizing simple shapes, with your eyes closed, or against a black surface, or briefly against a normally-lighted indoor or outdoor background.

- Three qualities are needed for successful Creative Visualization: Resolution, Concentration, Patience.

- Strengthen your motives for Creative Visualization by keeping your wishes at a high emotional pitch, and by sometimes re-living your daydreams.

Study Points

2

TENSION is the enemy of Creative Visualization.

1. As Human Beings, we must learn to relax *deliberately*, because:
    a. Our Instinctual Nature is only partially functioning.
    b. Our natural impulses and reactions are inhibited.
As a result, tensions are built up through a succession of frustrated emotions.

2. Tension is the natural prelude to purposeful action, but when that action is delayed or inhibited, tension builds up excessively, and may be only partially released. Such accumulated tensions lock up energies that are needed for powerful mental action.

3. A program of physical relaxation should lead to
    Wholeness ⎫   producing a true harmony
    Haleness ⎬   of body and psyche with
    Health   ⎭   well-being at all levels.

4. Creative Relaxation brings positive benefits to
    every part of the body with release of tension
    and free flow of energy. The Rhythmic Breath
    can boost energy, and direct it as required. The
    Rhythmic Breath should become a lifetime habit.

The Potent Circle

2

You have seen the importance of keeping your emotional motivation at a high pitch, so as to put the necessary drive and determination into your work for Creative Visualization.

One of the necessary qualities for success in Creative Visualization is *Concentration*, the ability to hold the mind effectively to one subject for a sufficient period; and a great enemy of concentration is physical and nervous tension.

Therefore we have to be sure, while maintaining the desired emotional motivation and drive, that the energy thus made available for your visualization purposes is not taken up wastefully and detrimentally in unwanted tensions of the muscles and of the nervous system.

How do these tensions arise?

In the wild world, there is little use for a pause between motivation and act. The deer catches a strange odor in the breeze, gets an impression of its type and nearness and is away instantly. The soaring eagle sees a slight movement below, the rhythm of the strong wings changes at once; the prey is located and the great bird plunges in the long dive to seize it. Delayed action spells *tension*: the tension of a cat stalking a mouse, the tension of a rabbit in a thicket awaiting the moment to bolt for safety.

It is also true, however, that among animals generally, when there is no crisis situation of any kind, there is no tension. A cat, for instance, stalking its prey is a different creature from a cat basking lazily on a ledge. A fish, even though it cannot close its eyes, can rest in complete peacefulness in the depths of its native water; the fins are perfectly poised, so that at the first need to find either safety or food, movement forward or back could be instantaneous.

Our basic pattern is just the same. *Tension is the natural prelude to purposeful action,* and ends when the action is performed; if the action cannot at once be performed, tension either fades or can become prolonged. In many sports we learn that alertness, readiness, watchfulness are not tension; but doubt, fear, inability to act adequately, or (just as in the stalking cat) an awareness that action, to be effective, must be delayed — these emotions permit tension to build up.

In some sports, such as boxing and fencing, it is quite important to be able to know in advance, if possible, when the opponent is planning a surprise move: in other words, when he is planning an action which "to be effective, must be delayed." So what do you look for? A sign of tension! And where do you look for it? Where any form of stress very readily shows: in the delicately-muscled tissue around the eyes.

The body so promptly follows out, or tries to follow out, what the mind is planning, that even those tiny muscles will, if they are allowed to do so, go into a pre-action state of tension. This is perfectly natural; but it can also be detrimental to the person concerned, by giving away the fact that he is planning something. So if he is keen on his particular form of sport, he will find it worthwhile to practice keeping a perfectly "dead-pan" face, a relaxed "mask" that will not change, whatever may be going through his mind. *This can in fact be done,* and a calm inscrutable face can be maintained through even the hottest pace and the closest contests.

It is the same with the card player. It is the same with the ballerina, dancing through the most intricate and strenuous movements, giving and taking cues that are timed to a split second, with an easy grace of body and an unchanging, trance-like look on her face. From this, we can see that no matter what is going on in the mind, *bodily relaxation can be achieved by a man or a woman who is resolved upon achieving it.* What can be done with the face, which is one of the areas of the body most responsive to emotional stimuli (causing smiles, frowns, laughter, questioning looks and a hundred other shades of expression) can certainly be done also with arms, legs, feet, hands and the rest of the body.

The reasons why we human beings, as distinct from other living creatures, need to relax deliberately, are twofold. In the first place, because of the great development and constant use of the reasoning faculties, most human beings (at least, civilized human beings; and there are few areas of the world in which people have not by this time been influenced to at least some extent by "civilized" ways of living and thinking) have their instinctual nature only partially functioning.

Furthermore, artificial living conditions, and the population increase (which means that more and more people are spending their entire lives in a completely human and man-made environment) are making it increasingly undesirable, and often downright impossible, for people follow out natural impulses spontaneously most of the time. It isn't "nice," for instance, to show anger or resentment to one's family and it would be the height of imprudence to show anger to one's fellow workers or to the boss; if a person feels like running away there is mostly nowhere to run to; only on certain recognized occasions is public joy or grief acceptable and then these emotions are supposed to be shown in standard ways. Much of this is inevitable; some of it may be in some ways even a good thing; but it does mean, for numbers of people every day, a succession of frustrated emotions, impulses which scarcely come into consciousness and certainly stand no chance of finding fulfillment in action. So there is a considerable build-up of unresolved tension.

This tends to produce a "vicious circle" because, as we have said, unresolved tension is entirely destructive to the qualities

RESOLUTION

CONCENTRATION

PATIENCE

by means of which a person CAN break through into fulfillment and make frustration a thing of the past.

Therefore, the first requisite is to learn to *relax*, and to practice relaxation as part of the daily life-style to win regular success in Creative Visualization.

In these *Llewellyn Practical Guides* you are not only being given valuable techniques and formulae as isolated items; you are also being given different parts of a *Way of Life* which is recognized, and has been recognized by teachers of Wisdom in different cultures and ages, as the best and surest life-style for people seeking to develop their inner faculties and to enrich their lives thereby. Because MOTIVATION, INCENTIVE, are essential considerations for anyone who looks at a possibility of making changes in the daily routine to which he or she was brought up, only those parts are being given in any one book which are most necessary to the practice which is set forth in that book. *That does not mean, however, that the recommendations in a particular book are only good in connection with the one practice.* They are ALL good as parts to build into the permanent life-style of anyone who is permanently interested in living FULLY as a human being.

Thus the practice of Relaxation which follows here is most valuable towards Creative Visualization, but even when you are altogether proficient in that art you will not want to give up your relaxation program; for it takes you toward that goal of *Wholeness, Haleness, Health,* the true harmony of body and psyche in the unity of the individual, which is so sound a basis for personal well-being at all levels.

Some people who always seem to have some little ailment or other are told by friends and neighbors, *"You think about yourself too much!"* They should be told, "You think about yourself IN A NEGATIVE WAY too much!" A famous Yogi, once when an interviewer asked him for the secret of his abundant health and prolonged youthfulness, replied,

"I CONTEMPLATE EVERY PART OF MY BODY IN TURN, AND WISH IT WELL!"

That is what you are going to do. *Creatively*.

The Creative Plan of Relaxation

(Enjoy this. Your body is not just one friend; your body is a whole crowd of friends. Some of them have their idiosyncrasies, their individual odd ways, but we don't have less affection for our friends on that account. They do a lot for you, sometimes without much thanks. Now you can get to know them better.)

Wear loose garments, or nothing. Be barefoot.

Lie flat on your back, as flat as you comfortably can. Draw your chin in slightly, rest on the back of your neck rather than the back of your head. If you really want to, you can put a soft but not too thick pad or cushion under your head. Let your arms lie slack, more or less parallel to your sides. Test what is going to happen when you relax your ankles: are your feet going to sag outwards uncomfortably? Don't let this make you cautious about relaxing them. Far better, arrange a couple of boxes or something, for them to come to rest against if and when they do sag outwards.

Lying thus, take a few deep, slow breaths. If by chance your body was not correctly and symmetrically settled, these breaths will probably be all that is needed to cause you to make any necessary adjustments. If you can, throughout this practice breathe gently, evenly and through your nostrils.

Now we can make a beginning with your right foot. Did you ever read Mark Twain's *A Connecticut Yankee in King Arthur's Court*? One episode concerns a pair of lovers who have been imprisoned in the dungeons for years, having no communication either with each other or with the outer world. The "Yankee" insists on their release, and evidently expects to see them rush into each other's arms. But this doesn't happen. Not only do they not recognize one another, they have evidently lost all power of communication. Certainly, the episode is a "tear-jerker," but in the pre-psychological era in which the book was written, it was a good indication of Mark Twain's perceptiveness and originality that he realized what the outcome would be. To be imprisoned in isolation, to be forgotten and denied means of communication, does indeed tend to produce apathy, with an increasing slowness and then real loss of the means to communicate or to respond to a change of conditions.

But who, in these days, would be so unheeding of the welfare of prisoners? *A lot of people are — when the prisoners are feet and toes!*

Even on vacation, when you can go barefoot or wear sandals, do you give any attention, any notice to your feet? (This is not just a matter of trimming your toenails, although there too you have an opportunity for something further.) If you *do* take notice of these poor "underdogs," if you give them a place in the sun, have friendly communication with them and respect their needs — excellent! You will find the first part of this relaxation practice proportionately easy. If, however, you have consistently ignored them for years, just pushed them around, in fact, they may not at once be able to respond perceptibly to your new attitude of friendship towards them. *Persevere, however.*

Wriggle the toes of your right foot; see how many of them you can move individually, and to what extent. Really try, mentally, to get each one to signal its response to your message. This may take some concentration. (Don't spend long enough over it to exhaust either your energy or your time, but if the results have not been entirely satisfactory give your toes a few minutes attention from time to time during the day. From the point of view of personal development you will find this eminently worthwhile.) Relax the toes.

Next, still keeping your heel on the ground, bring your right foot "upward" (that is, flex it towards your head) so that you feel the muscles stretch in the calf and contract on the front of the shin. Do this a few times, directing a thought of encouragement and approval to the muscles, tendons and nerves which are doing the work. "Clench" all the toes together, keeping the knee straight: relax them, then repeat several times. Relax.

Lifting your heel now from the ground, and keeping your right knee straight, see how far towards the vertical you can bring your right leg *without bending your left knee either!* While the right leg is thus raised, rotate the foot on the ankle, about six times clockwise and then six times counter-clockwise. Consider with goodwill the various components — you can probably feel some of them moving — which are taking part in this action. Lower the leg slowly, relax, then raise it again and repeat the lifting to (or towards) vertical, the rotation in both directions, the slow lowering. *Is your* left *knee still straight?*

Relax your right leg totally: toes, foot, ankle, calf and shin muscles, knee, thigh muscles, buttock. Goodwill, strength and blessing to your right leg!

Repeat the entire performance with your left toes, foot and leg. When you have concluded this, sending messages of friendship and benevolence to every part that you can distinguish, check that *both* legs are now fully relaxed. Goodwill, strength and blessing to your left leg!

We proceed to the very important abdominal region. While it is certainly true that every part of your body will respond to the positive and benevolent thoughts you are now directing to them individually, there is in certain parts of the body a capacity for something nearer to a *conscious* response; the highly specialized internal organs are in this latter category, both those in the abdomen and those in the chest. Although in this relaxation practice it is only possible to bring into deliberate action the "voluntary" muscles of the limbs and trunk (there are more than 600 of them!), the internal organs, whose muscles are "involuntary" and thus are linked more closely to the instinctual and emotional areas of the psyche, will be especially responsive to the feeling-charged thoughts which you will now be sending them.

So while you are using and relaxing the outer muscles of the abdomen, direct a specific well-wishing thought to each of the organs inside them: the liver and gall-bladder, the stomach with its glands, the spleen, intestines, kidneys, bladder and sex organs. Try not to forget any! In fact, a very deep psychological truth, or an inseparable pair of truths, is involved here, with regard to your ability to direct these specific thought-wishes to the individual organs:

WE CAN ONLY TRULY KNOW THAT WHICH WE LOVE. WE CAN ONLY TRULY LOVE THAT WHICH WE KNOW.

You may, therefore, feel you could do this part of the practice better if you knew more about the internal organs, the work they do for you and their location inside your body. If this is the case, a good "family health" or medical book will help you to some valuable knowledge: better still, attend if you can a series of first aid classes and so gain your knowledge in a way that may be valuable to others besides yourself, thus giving very practical form to your benevolence towards the body.

The abdominal muscles can be considered in two

sets, dividing at about the navel. The muscles of the lower abdomen have already been given some activity by you, in raising and lowering your legs, but if you feel like it you can do this again (raise the right leg with the knee straight, as nearly vertical as you can without moving the left leg; then raise the left leg similarly, then each leg once more), this time *thinking of the abdominal muscles employed rather than the legs*. Now relax. Flex the lumbar muscles (small of the back), relax; repeat this too a few times.

Now take a deep breath — deeper than you have normally been taking during this practice, letting the air well into the lower part of the lungs so that the higher part of the abdomen distends. (Girls, you may need some extra practice in this because your ribs are especially flexible and so your chest naturally accommodates the air you breathe in. But this practice of making sure the lower part of the lungs is filled, is good for you!) Having taken this breath in, hold it while you *contract* the muscles of the upper abdomen, thus sending the air into the chest proper and expanding the ribs. Then breathe out. Don't hold the breath uncomfortably long; the main purpose is to give the upper abdominal muscles something to push against while you are contracting them. And don't do this set of movements (or, indeed, any of the movements) violently or jerkily.

Repeat this several times. Relax the muscles of the upper abdomen. Check too that those of the lower abdomen and of the legs are still relaxed.

The next part of the body to be considered is the chest, and here, besides the muscles that you will actually be employing, your thoughts should be directed to your heart and lungs. A deep and intimate feeling for and with these very responsive organs (but avoiding any shade of anxiety) should infuse your understanding of their incessant and unsleeping work for you. *Be inspired* with the Breath of Life; and *be of good heart,* confident, optimistic and resolute!

Slowly take a deep breath; but this time, instead of expanding the chest further by simply moving the air already taken into the lungs, when the lungs seem fully expanded *gently compel them to take in a little more air* so that you can feel this extra air being sucked in. Next, breathe out gently, as far as you normally can; then by a contraction in the region of the diaphragm (at the bottom of the rib-cage) *drive out a little more air,* emptying the lungs even further. Now breathe in your ordinary manner, letting the chest muscles relax. Repeat this procedure about three times more.

Flex the pectoral muscles (tensing your elbows in towards your sides), relax. Press the shoulder-blades back, then relax. Contract the neck muscles, relax. Repeat a few times for pectorals, shoulders, neck; then relax. Be happily aware for a little while of your heart beating, of the rhythm of your breathing.

Goodwill, strength and blessing to your body and to all the vital organs within it!

Raise your right forearm just enough so you can
look at your right hand without effort; keep the elbow
on the ground. Straighten the right hand, extend all the
fingers, then flex them one at a time. As you did with
your toes, try to move each finger quite individually.
Then do the same with the thumb. Stretch the thumb
across the palm as far as you can; touch the base of the
little finger with the ball of the thumb if this is possible
for you. Relax. Straighten the hand.

Now bend the hand as far forward on the wrist as
you can, keeping the fingers straight. Now bend it as
far back as you can. Repeat this several times, being
aware of the stretching and contracting muscles of the
arm in each instance. Try circling the hand upon the
wrist, with as smooth a movement as possible, clockwise, then counter-clockwise. Be aware of the various
components — bones, muscles, tendons, nerves —
involved in this movement; then relax. Think of the
various skills you have achieved, the various actions
you perform with this hand. (There ought to be *some*,
even if you are left-handed, just as a right-handed person
really ought to make the effort to learn to use the left
hand to some extent. Suppose for instance you were
to sprain the wrist of your more able hand, how many
of your normal daily activities could you still carry
out? But still, be grateful for all this hand can do!)

Raise the right arm vertically from the ground,
forming a right angle at the elbow; clench the fist

(thumb outside) as hard as you can, bend the clenched fist forward upon the wrist, flex the biceps. Relax; repeat several times, feeling the triceps muscle stretch as the biceps contracts; relax, unclench the hand, return the arm to the side. Repeat with the left arm and hand.

Now check that all the muscles previously used are relaxed: feet, legs, thighs, abdomen, back, chest, shoulders, neck, fingers, hands, forearms, upper arms.

Clench the jaw, press the eyelids together; then gently relax. Think what wonderful organs are your eyes, ears, nose, mouth; what wonderful means of expression are your vocal apparatus, tongue and lips. Think how much can be conveyed by a smile: smile now, beginning with those delicate muscles around the eyes, feeling peaceful and happy as you contract them, letting your mouth be caught up into the expression so that the lips finally part in a smile of pure joy. Why not? Here is another great secret we can learn from the mystics of East and West alike:

SEPARATE YOURSELF, IF ONLY FOR A MO-MENT, FROM THE CARES, WORRIES, FEARS, PAINS OR REGRETS THAT BESET YOU, *AND YOU WILL KNOW THAT YOUR REAL SELF IS PURE JOY!*

That is the true reason why relaxation helps you to be resolute, to concentrate, to have patience.

Having come to the final point in this practice, RELAX totally, with closed eyes, peaceful face, body and limbs heavy and easy. Stay like that, gently breathing, listening to your heart beating, for a few minutes before you think of returning to ordinary activity. Goodwill, strength and blessing to your brain and nervous system, to your head and countenance, to your faculties of sight, hearing, smell, taste and touch! Goodwill, strength and blessing to every part!

That is the Creative Plan of Relaxation. You may very likely wish to personalize it by adding something for a particular need or interest of your own; that is a very good thing to do, and you only have to take care *to work it into the harmony of the whole.* This relaxation practice, simply and carefully performed, can benefit you very considerably; it will help you towards Creative Visualization, because it will assist you in developing greatly your powers of

RESOLUTION

CONCENTRATION

PATIENCE

— but then, imagine the splendid effect of Creative Visualization upon your Creative Relaxation Plan! Instead of a "vicious circle," you now have a "Potent Circle!" — because as you bring into awareness, and then relax, each part of your body in turn, *you will make your well-wishing many times more powerful by visualizing that same part RADIANT WITH HEALTH!*

There is another technique which is important in developing and maintaining the qualities you need for repeated success in Creative Visualization. It is so directly important that we give it here, even though it has already been given in *The Llewellyn Practical Guide to Astral Projection*. Obviously it would not be fair if we were to repeat a great deal of material from one book to another. In the *Astral Projection* book there is, for instance, advice on diet, physical exercise and other topics which are of great basic value to anyone wishing to take seriously the development of ANY OR ALL of his or her inner faculties, but we cannot reasonably keep repeating all the general counsel, sound and well-founded though we know it to be. The technique which follows, however, is related just as specifically to Creative Visualization as it is to Astral Projection, and this present book would not be complete without it.

Rhythmic Breath

In acquiring this simple technique, the purpose is to become accustomed to it so that it can be practiced AT WILL, and can then be continued without repeatedly giving attention to it. This frequently fails to occur with untrained breathing; any student with experience of intense mental work, whether philosophic or creative, may know the frustration of having his attention snatched away, his concentration destroyed, by the discovery that he has unconsciously left off breathing.

Besides, Rhythmic Breath establishes a rhythm which is *natural to the individual,* so that when words have to be uttered, for instance (or actions performed, as in the Creative Plan of Relaxation), these can easily be fitted into the pattern of breathing, and with a little practice all is brought into a personal, natural and EFFECTIVE harmony.

The first step is to become aware of your heartbeat, verifying this if necessary by feeling the pulse in your throat, temples or wrist. *Begin counting your heartbeats.*

Now fill your lungs with air, as full as you COMFORTABLY can. Hold your breath for *three* heartbeats.

Breathe out in a steady and controlled manner during *six* heartbeats.

Keep your lungs empty during *three* heartbeats.

Breathe in steadily during *six.*

And so on. Try this a few times to get the feel of it, smoothly and steadily.

You may find it is just a matter of practice to get used to this rhythm, or you may feel sure this particular timing does not suit you. You may find, for instance, that you need a longer time to fill or empty your lungs. Alternatively, you may find three heartbeats an uncomfortably long time to hold your breath. *Good; that sort of discovery was the purpose of this first experiment!*

What you are aiming to establish is a pattern of breathing in which you can comfortably hold your lungs full of air for a certain number of heartbeats, then breathe OUT during *twice* that number of heartbeats so that your lungs are as empty as you can comfortably make them; then breathe IN during the count of the double number, your lungs being well expanded at the end. Almost certainly, you will find after some practice that you can settle comfortably with one or another of the following examples:

Hold lungs full during	Breathe out during	Hold lungs empty during	Breathe in during
2 beats	4 beats	2 beats	4 beats
3 beats	6 beats	3 beats	6 beats
4 beats	8 beats	4 beats	8 beats

For the present purpose, it is of no consequence *which* of these you choose; just take the one that you can use most comfortably. After some time, you are in any case likely to find that your capacity increases: for instance, you may begin with 2-4-2-4 and find after awhile that your breathing capacity now allows you to change to 3-6-3-6. That's fine — but *you must* in all cases *keep to the rhythm of the breath*; until you can comfortably hold your breath both IN and

OUT for three heartbeats, you should not extend your time of inhaling or exhaling over six heartbeats. Wait until after another week's practice, and most likely you will then find you can use the 3-6-3-6 rhythm correctly and comfortably.

So experiment, but keep always to the pattern given. To have a breathing rhythm of 1-2-1-2, or of 5-10-5-10, would be unusual but quite in order. But always have your time of inhaling and of exhaling *double* the number of heartbeats during which you hold your breath in or out. And *always count by your own heartbeats!* If you have an audible watch or clock, put it where you can't hear it while you practice.

The principles of Rhythmic Breath are used in all parts of the world, and in different ways for different purposes. To alter the basic plan you have been given would be like experimenting blindly with a Morse key — or with a jungle drum! But equally, the rewards for building up with practice to a good, steady, dependable Rhythmic Breath which you can sustain indefinitely, are very great. Use it when doing your relaxation and Creative Visualization practices, when going to sleep, and during any physical or mental work. It can boost energy, and it can *direct* energy.

PRACTICE
RHYTHMIC BREATHING
UNTIL IT BECOMES A HABIT
AND MAKE IT AN ALLY FOR LIFE

Checkpoint

2

• Practice the Creative Plan of Relaxation daily until you are proficient at it. After that, still continue daily if you feel you need it, if you are following any procedure given later in this book which calls for it, or just because you enjoy it. If you give up doing it daily, try to make it three days a week.

• Should you feel it will help you in the needed visualization and well-wishing, find out more about the body's different structures and functions.

• Continue practicing simple visualization (as outlined in the preceding chapter) if you need to, but don't let it delay your beginning the other practices in the book. You will find there is much you can do before you are fully proficient in visualization; besides, incentive will grow with progress, and proficiency will be hastened by incentive. You'll realize *what visualization does and why it is vitally important.*

• Practice Rhythmic Breathing whenever and wherever you can, whatever you may be doing meanwhile; but especially when doing Visualization, Creative Relaxation, or any other self-development procedure.

Study Points

3

Rhythmic Breathing gives FORCE & FORM to whatever you are doing.

We are all part of the Universe, and the only thing that keeps us from filling our needs from its abundance is the unconscious feeling of deprivation that many have. When you "re-program" the Unconscious Mind, this inhibition is removed.

In seeking to develop your Inner Faculties, you are making contact with the UNCONSCIOUS levels of your psyche.
   a.   The Unconscious levels are the *irresponsible* levels.
   b.   You must assert control over these levels from the Rational Mind.

c.   Associate JOY with images of the things you desire, and SING ABOUT THEM! Song appeals to the emotions, getting through to the Unconscious levels.

You Have a Great Future!

3

At first you may wonder how the procedure of Rhythmic Breathing can possibly keep your mind OFF that function. Don't worry about it! If you use this technique faithfully as it is given in the previous chapter, the day will come when you have to give careful thought, planning or calculation to something, and you will realize after some time *that you have switched into Rhythmic Breathing without thinking about it, and have been breathing that way for maybe half an hour!*

From the beginning, however, you can and should build it into your visualization practices, whether these are simple experiments in visualization or actual Creative Visualization operations. You will find that going along with this basic rhythm (which is in any case a part of your own life) helps at once in giving form and force to whatever you are doing.

You can now organize your practice times in an orderly way. What times are you going to set apart for your Creative Visualization? Early morning is the best; if you can choose this, you are making an excellent start to the day, making your first activity a move towards your real objectives or at least towards your next goal! Last thing at night is also very good indeed, since it probably will cause your unconscious mind (the level you really want to involve) to carry on while you are asleep the creative activity you have begun while awake. And the third choice, which is not so powerful, *if used alone,* is around noon.

If you can manage two, or three, of these times daily instead of just one, that is better still; but it is advisable to settle for something you can manage REGULARLY, instead of depending on haphazard moments.

In all cases, if you intend to carry out this activity while seated, sit on a firm chair, be relaxed but have the spine vertical (this is largely a matter of balance), and place the soles of your feet side by side upon the floor. Rest your palms easily upon your thighs, except when you may want to make some special movement with your hands (as may occur quite naturally during your visualization activity). For visualization last thing at night, it is best, if you are also having a Creative Relaxation session, to do your relaxation *before going to bed*, and preferably lying on a comfortable rug; but do your visualization *in bed*.

For visualization activity while lying down, lie on your back, as flat as you can. Of course, if you need a high pillow for other reasons (for instance, if you are a bronchial sufferer), then you must keep to this; but if you can easily habituate yourself to using a low pillow, this is better for Creative Visualization and, indeed, for ANY effort to develop the inner faculties. The reason is not far to seek: the brain is a "greedy" organ, and if it is to function properly, especially with regard to its less accustomed activities, it must have a good blood-supply. We do our best to starve it by sitting upright all day, whereas our ancient ancestors in all cultures would have spent a good part of their leisure reclining; we should at least do our best to make up for this and to give the brain a fair share of the circulation while we sleep.

You should also have, during the night, *a good supply of air.* If this means that you also have too much light coming into your room, from the moon or from traffic or from flashing electric signs, then obtain or make for yourself an *eye-shield.* This useful article is, essentially, like a carnival mask with no holes for the eyes; it is narrow, lightweight, and is kept in place by an elastic passing around the back of the head. A small black shield of this description also has the advantage of not being too strange or startling to your spouse, or to a friend or relative who might in some emergency enter the room.

Having settled yourself, then, comfortably on your back in a well-ventilated darkness, or being seated at morning or noonday in a balanced and easy posture, your next step will be to commence Rhythmic Breath. Let this continue for at least ten complete breaths (more if you feel like it) before going on with your visualization activities, whether these be simple visualization practice or creative work.

Keep the Rhythmic Breath going while you proceed with your visualization. Soon you will quite easily find ways to combine the two activities. For instance, if you are doing simple visualization, you might while breathing IN check over mentally the characteristics of the shape you intend to visualize (if a triangle, are all its sides of the same length? — how wide are the angles? — where is the apex to be placed? If a star, how many points has it? — does it have a point at the top, or a valley? etc.). Then while holding the breath, let this "germinate;" and while breathing OUT, visualize it. On the next breath IN, let it fade; wait, then reformulate it. As a first simple step in Creative Visualization, you should visualize your image (say a house) while breathing IN; hold it steady while holding the breath; then, breathing OUT, say mentally appropriate words, such as "My—house, my—house!" Less banal examples of suitable words may come to your mind, but *always check them over carefully before you use them, in case you find yourself saying something you don't mean!*

This kind of accident is particularly likely to happen to people who are trying in any way to develop their inner faculties; it is tiresome and can even be dangerous to their plans, because when it occurs, people find they are peculiarly liable to get what they SAID, rather than what they MEANT. (For instance, there was a man who repeated over and over, "I want a new house!" mentally adding, "Then I can marry my girl," until suddenly he caught himself repeating, "I want a new girl!")

Why does it happen?

The reason why the wrong thing is said, and the reason why this is so often the very thing that "comes true," are one and the same. In seeking to develop your inner faculties, you are, rightly, making contact with the unconscious levels of your psyche.

The unconscious levels are the irresponsible levels. A small child in whom the reasoning faculty is not yet developed, or a mentally sick person in whom it is dormant, or a sleep-walker, cannot be held *responsible* for what they do, because in all those cases, for different reasons, the unconscious levels of the psyche are in control.

But the unconscious levels are also the effective levels for getting what you want. Look at an animal, and see how well it is adapted to its own habitat and life-style. No animal could possibly have worked it all out deliberately! — nor would just "knowing" by conscious human-style reasoning have obtained what they wanted.

The deer have extra air-passages near the inner corner of the eyes, so that when running at high speed they can obtain more air to breathe than the nostrils can take in. Young animals of many kinds are dappled or striped, even though their elders may be of one plain color; the babies need the extra concealment of looking like the dappled or striped light-effects in the dells or brakes in which they rest. A flat-fish when newly hatched swims like an angel fish, but spends its adult life lying on its side on the sea-bed. It has one eye move over before that change, so that both are on the upper side of the head. Countless adaptations could be named: the eyes of the cat, the hoofs of the horse, the dead-leaf color and shape of a butterfly's wings when folded, are within our frequent observation.

Plainly, this phenomenon merits our attention.

Darwin tried to explain it by pointing out that when some animals of a particular kind had a particular protective or helpful device, and others did not, the "improved model" animals would tend to survive better than the others. This is sound as far as it goes, but it does nothing to explain *how the improvement arose in the first place*. Neither does the "all-wise Providence" idea quite work, because the unconscious psychic levels which look after these things, whether for human or for other creatures, *are NOT "all-wise."*

Take the case of the prehistoric Irish Elk.

We can't say that the Irish Elk (whose bones have been found in other regions, but Ireland and Denmark harbored the largest ones) "wished," in the human way of wishing, to be taller or to have larger antlers. We can't say exactly by what physical process the thing was achieved, but it could probably be analyzed as a combined nutritional and glandular effect. Clearly, it was an advantage — *up to a point* — that the stags should be as large, and have as powerful antlers, as possible, to defend the herd from wolves, bears and other predators; and we can add, for the sake of the Darwinists, that these mighty stags (*when once the trend had set in*) would doubtless defeat the smaller ones in the mating season contests. All these factors would work together, so that in due course the male Irish Elk became, as a fact, a massive creature whose antlers — great sheets of horn with protruding points at the edges — were sometimes as much as *thirteen feet from tip to tip.*

Then the Irish Elks slowly died out, the largest strains first. Why? Scientists have varied in their opinions, but the story in any case centers upon *those antlers.* The likeliest version seems to be that living in forest areas, as the huge creatures virtually had to do, so as to obtain sufficient vegetation as food, the tremendously wide antlers made speed or ease of movement impossible; the stags were unable to defend the herd, and became an easy prey themselves.

So, work WITH the unconscious levels of the psyche to obtain what you see would be good for you, but BEWARE OF LETTING THEM TAKE THE CONTROLS! As an individual, YOU NEED YOUR RATIONAL MIND IN CHARGE, *to keep your sub-rational and material natures from running into trouble.*

This is not to say that your rational mind is the highest faculty your psyche possesses. Strictly, IT IS NOT; and as you proceed further and further in the development of your inner powers, you should gradually become more aware of the existence and the living reality of your Higher Self. You have, however, to be able to proceed *effectively* and *safely* before this awareness comes.

So in your Creative Visualization program: PLAN what you are going to

visualize

say silently

say aloud.

DON'T ACT ON IMPULSE during visualization sessions. THINK CAREFULLY of all the implications before making any changes in your plan for visualization.

AT ALL OTHER TIMES DURING YOUR WAKING DAY, remain silent about your visualization program — but, as far as possible, THINK, SPEAK and ACT harmoniously to it.

REMEMBER — YOU HAVE A GREAT FUTURE!

Let's say that again:—

YOU HAVE A GREAT FUTURE!

The certainty of this will help you keep control of the unconscious levels of the psyche *now.*

Much of the trouble with "demand-and-supply" in this world is due to so many people feeling (for one reason and another) at a deep level *disinherited,* so that when they begin to gain something their subrational nature takes control and they "can't stop."

This is partly a result of a sophistication which has caused our emotional and instinctual nature to feel "inferior" and "deprived," and in many cases has really diminished our sense of unity with the world around us, the universe in which we live.

Such a diminished sense of unity, however, is one of the things we should be able in time to put right by our Creative Visualization. For *of course* we are an integral part of the world, and we are never, NOT EVER, going to "fall out of the universe;" so we need only take from its abundance at any time what we see to be good for us.

That is an important fact. People who have felt (for whatever reason) DEPRIVED of this or that, need to realize that they are an integral part of the world and to alter their feeling RIGHT THROUGH TO THE UNCONSCIOUS LEVELS OF THE PSYCHE. Otherwise, when they meet with Plenty, *no amount of "will-power" is likely to keep them from SNATCHING childishly at the thing they felt deprived of, or a substitute thing.* This is because in such a case the emotional-instinctual levels, *which are sub-rational,* HAVE TAKEN CONTROL.

So when you have chosen WHAT YOU REALLY WANT IN LIFE, and what fits in with your real plans, *direct the attention of your emotional nature to the attractions of those things.* Don't let it wander into GREEDINESS for things of which you want only a limited amount, nor into WASTING ITS CAPACITY FOR DESIRE (which is YOUR capacity for desire) over unimportant, irrelevant or contrary objects. *But be sure to allow yourself MAXIMUM PLEASURE in thinking about, dwelling upon, the things which* are *part of your plans for the future;* and then the less important pleasures can very well fit into the scene *in their proper place.*

One way of dwelling upon, delighting in, the thing you want is, certainly, the "image" or "picture" method that has been mentioned. But besides that — *Do the most joyful thing we are capable of doing:* SING ABOUT IT! Never mind what your voice is like — *you can do this.* You could even do this without uttering a sound, and in some circumstances you might choose indeed not to utter a sound but just to sing mentally, sing in your imagination. It would still be well worth doing.

SING ABOUT IT!

If you want something like rural quiet, or a home in this or that region, or something such as "A Room with a View for Two," ideas which have always appealed to song-writers, you will have very little trouble here (although even so you should beware of "negative" words and ideas which may need weeding out; up to this century, poets and song-writers were a melancholy lot!). If, however, you want something that has been less romanticized, you will need to do more adapting. But you are not going to sing your composition on a concert platform; you will probably only sing the words when you are alone, and otherwise just hum or whistle a phrase or so of the melody while you "think" the words.

So you don't have to be a genius to take a tune that comes into your head, and alter the words to say as plainly as possible what you mean. You might think of "There is a Tavern in the Town," or "Home on the Range," or "Jeanie with the Light Brown Hair," and sing, according to your wants,

I'm going to get my Ph.D. — Ph.D. —
To open just the door for me — door for me —
or
I'll have me a shape that's slim by the tape,
And pleasant to see on the beach!
or even
It's mine, that Moped with the two-HP engine!

But take a melody YOU like, and set YOUR wish to it!

You'll notice that in each of the examples just given, brief and simple though these are, there is someting special by way of incentive: the usefulness of the degree, the pleasure of looking good on the beach, the sheer pride of ownership.

There is a great deal to be said for the "It's mine!" attitude in these chants, on two conditions:

(1) You have to be able to believe it: it is true, ASTRALLY, when once you have visualized the thing or the fact strongly enough to put it there. (We shall say more about this in the next chapter.)

(2) This "realization" must HELP you, not HINDER you, in doing whatever may be needed towards *bringing it through to the material level* — for instance, studying for the degree, putting money aside (if possible) for the machine, dieting sensibly for the slimmer shape.

Suitable actions on the material level, *when you are in a position to do them,* MUST be done because it is in the material world that you want your "dream come true." CREATIVE VISUALIZATION IS TO TAKE CARE OF THE FACTORS YOU *CAN'T* CONTROL — being ready for the very questions in the exam, keeping your mind *off* the enjoyment of fattening foods, having little "windfalls" come along to help towards whatever you are saving for AND FIRMLY KEEPING THEM FOR THAT PURPOSE. It can, and will, do much more surprising things for you than these, *but we can't generalize about them.*

These things are so individual, IT WILL BE AS IF THEY CAME BY MAIL, *WITH YOUR NAME ON THEM!*

Checkpoint

3

- Make a time-table so you can practice Creative Visualization REGULARLY.

- Visualization practice at night is best done when you are in bed, but make your sleeping conditions as helpful as possible.

- Choose what you really want in life, and direct your emotional nature towards it.

- You can combine spoken words with your Rhythmic Breath to aid Creative Visualization:
    Breathing in — visualize the image
    Holding breath — Contemplate the image
    Breathing out — Speak affirmation of what you
                are visualizing.

- Make a song about it; to change the words of an existing song is easy, and will keep you in mind of your wish.

Study Points

4

There are four levels of human existence:
1. The Higher Self: The Divine Flame, of which we are mostly unaware.
2. Rational Consciousness: which is responsible for the welfare of the Lower Self.
3. The Emotional & Instinctual Nature: of which we are aware when it expresses itself in emotion, but which is otherwise largely submerged in the Lower Unconscious.
4. The Physical Body: including the brain, sense organs, and nervous system.

There are four corresponding levels to the external Universe:
1. World of the Divine: in which the Higher Self functions.

2. Intellectual World: in which the Rational Consciousness functions.
3. Astral World: in which the Emotional & Instinctual Nature functions.
4. Material World: in which the physical body functions.

We exist and function at *every level of the Universe* — even though our Conscious Mind is only aware of a small part:

a. We actually are acting at levels where we have no personal consciousness.
b. In order to act with "unity" (without inhibiting factors), we have to gain the cooperation of the unconscious levels.
c. Each level can act with or upon the level immediately above or below it.
d. The higher the level at which we can act, the more sure and permanent the effects will be.

To fill yourself with LIGHT is to experience a beginning of contact with the Higher Self.

The Life-Sustaining Flow

4

This is an extremely important chapter.

Every chapter in this book is important, but when you have read, and well digested and understood, this chapter, you will see more deeply into all the rest of the book.

At the same time, you will more clearly understand *this* chapter, because you have now seen what Chapters 1, 2 and 3 are about.

By Creative Visualization you can achieve, or possess, whatever you truly want in life.

So can EVERYBODY who, knowingly or unknowingly, applies the principles.

So where does this plenty come from? And how? And *by what right* do we claim it?

You must understand, and be easy in your mind about, the answers to these questions.

Because the better you understand the principles, the more smoothly you will be able to VISUALIZE their working — and so the better they will work for you.

And also because any *lurking doubts* in your mind would put weights in the contrary side of the balance AGAINST your effective operation. And we don't want *any* weights — even small ones — to find their way into that contrary side of the balance.

You, as a human being, exist on four different levels simultaneously:

There is your HIGHER SELF, your purely spiritual nature, which is in essence *divine* (the Divine Flame) but of which most of us are in everyday life unaware (the Higher Unconscious, the Intuitive Mind, the Higher Faculties), but which is *present* in each individual.

There is your RATIONAL CONSCIOUSNESS, which ought to be *receptive to* any awareness of the Higher Self, but which has, subject to that, to be actively *responsible for* the welfare of your whole *lower self*.

There is your EMOTIONAL AND INSTINCTUAL NATURE, of which you are *conscious* when it expresses itself in emotion, but which is otherwise largely submerged in the *Lower Unconscious* (which also acts in co-ordination with the involuntary nerves).

Finally, there is your PHYSICAL BODY, of which the brain, sense organs and nervous systems are a part.

The external universe is also conceived of as being made up of four levels, which correspond to the four levels in a human being. (Fairly obviously, *if there are* any other levels in the external universe, since we are limited to human perception on the subject we are probably unable to be aware of those other levels.) There is the WORLD OF THE DIVINE — the God-world — in which our highest nature is at home. There is the INTELLECTUAL WORLD, in which our mental, rational nature is at home. There is the ASTRAL WORLD, in which our emotional and instinctual nature is at home. And there is the MATERIAL WORLD, in which our physical bodies are at home.

So YOU — and every other person — have an existence which extends through every level of the universe, even though your conscious mind is aware of only a small part of the universe.

That immediately shows you the GREAT IMPORTANCE of having the co-operation of *the unconscious levels* in your activities. This enables you to operate at levels of which you have *no personal consciousness*: rather as scientists can receive observations and samples by means of instruments on other planets or in the depths of the sea, even though the scientists have no personal sensations of seeing, hearing, digging or scraping when the instruments are performing those actions.

But in our activities, the "instruments" are a living part of us; to gain awareness of them, as our inner development gradually continues, will be a most valuable part — in fact, THE most valuable part — of our development.

To understand how Creative Visualization "works," however, we need to consider some facts of the Mystery Traditions concerning the external universe also.

Each level in the individual person can interact with its corresponding level in the external universe. We can dig in our material garden. Our emotions stir the Astral Light. Mentally, we can act in the Intellectual World. If we can contact the Divine Spark in ourselves, we are in touch with the Divine Mind.

Each level of the universe can act upon, or with, the level immediately above or below it. These levels are not, indeed, separated by clear-cut boundaries. (For comparison, imagine a stream flowing over earth. Above the solid earth there is mud, then turbid water, then clear water. In the surface-water there are many air-bubbles, then above that there is spray-filled air, then above that there is clear air.)

The Mental World emanates from the World of the Divine and is receptive to it: it also acts upon and influences the Astral World. The Astral World emanates from the Mental World, but also receives vibrations from the Material World. The Material World emanates from, and is directly influenced by, the Astral World.

We can, fairly easily, create impulses and images and "implant" them in the Astral World.

We can, by mind-power and concentration, cause these impulses and images in the Astral World to become "infused" with the power of the Mental World. As this power remains part of the Mental World, our impulses and images now have their counterpart at a purely mental level.

We cannot directly "cause" any action from the Divine World (at least, not until we are high adepts, mystics of the kind known as *thaumaturgists,* "wonder-workers"). However, if we work suitably we can create a "channel" through which Divine Power may act in the Mental World, and we know if this channel is right and congenial — archetypal — it will not be refused. Then, if the contacts are continuous, this action will naturally have its effect in the Astral World (because the Mental World is "causal" to the Astral World) and this in turn will have its effect in the Material World.

But, since we are able to implant impulses and images in the Astral World, can we not simply depend on these, without going further, to reflect back and cause the changes we want in the material world?

Creative Visualization is sometimes used in this way, but then it is likely to cause only weak, transitory results in the material world.

THE HIGHER THE LEVEL AT WHICH WE CAN
SET IN MOTION A DESIRED ACTION, THE SURER
AND MORE PERMANENT ITS EFFECTS WILL BE.

The medieval mystics knew this. Changes which
were set in motion at only astral level, they despised as
the work of those who either lacked the knowledge to go
higher, or for moral reaons DARED NOT. To the weak
and transitory effects of merely astral-level operation
they gave the name of "glamor" — a word which has a
rather different meaning nowadays, but which still
defines an effect, an attractiveness, whose causes
whether physical, instinctual or emotional are altogether
the concern of the material and astral worlds.

It is important to YOU, then, that you should:—

(a) KNOW HOW TO bring into your Creative Visualization programs those higher levels which will make their
results *lasting and reliable*.

(b) UNDERSTAND THE ETHICS of Creative Visualization so that you need have no hesitations, reservations
or hidden guilt-feelings which would cripple or maybe
even prevent your efforts to contact those higher levels.

All the rest of this book is devoted to the HOW-TO
aspects of various forms of practice in Creative Visualization. But the ETHICS need dealing with *now*.

We have seen how all the levels of the universe interact and how they are, indeed, intermingled and united. There is no sharp division between "spirit" and "matter," for the plain reason that in this whole scheme of things, sharp divisions are not at any level normal and, in fact, rarely exist.

Even at the Equator, there is a brief time from the beginning to the completion of the sun's appearance above the horizon, or his disappearance below it; a brief twilight, softening the change between night and day. Amphibious mammals exist in many regions, and there are walking and climbing fish. There are animal-like plants and plant-like animals. Not to digress too far into a fascinating theme, *boundaries are "out;"* the parts of the world and of the universe are interwoven in a united whole, just as a man from his highest spirit to his physical body is one individual. You could be emotionally depressed, and have your mental processes colored, by a physical pain; while a serious bodily sickness can often be overcome by spiritual joy, confidence or strength, your own or someone else's (for between one individual and another the boundaries are not rigid either).

The physicists nowadays are telling us what the mystics have always known: that everything which exists, even the densest matter, consists of nothing but *energy*. AND WHAT IS ENERGY?

Fortunately we do not need to pursue that question further than the dictionary definitions, which can be generally summed up as "power or activity, or the ability to exert power or activity." The point is, YOU are characterized by the ability to exert power or activity — you are doing that all your life, if only by breathing and by a ceaseless stream of mental activity — and you are at home in a universe which, spiritually and materially, has the same characteristic. (Even a piece of lead, or of glass, is made up of atoms which, with their components, are in an intense state of activity.)

So what is the point in saying, as some folk try to tell us, that we should only use our physical-plane powers to obtain material things, and should keep our spiritual powers for obtaining spiritual things?

In any case, to do physical work effectively we need all our wits about us; while for mental work, we need all the energy that sensible diet and rest (the right amount of the right kinds, in both cases) can give us. In this, again, THE PERSON IS A SINGLE UNIT.

The real trouble, for a good many people, is a result of taking certain passages in the New Testament right out of context, and trying to make that few words a rule of life. Taking words out of context is in any case an unfair way to treat any book, and especially one so complex as the New Testament. Indeed, the existence of four Gospels suggests a balancing of components.

Our first requirement if we are going to consider such a passage is to put the New Testament as a whole "into context," by considering the sort of people to whom it was initially addressed.

They were people of the Eastern Mediterranean, chiefly Jews and Greeks, acutely intelligent, but on the whole rougher, tougher and less sensitive than their present-day counterparts.

They also had, however, the virtues of their failings. They were fairly sure — Greeks, Jews or other civilized persons of those regions — that their God or Gods would look after such needs as they might specify in the approved manner, even though the "approved manner" was likely to be a traditional form quite inexpressive of their particular identity or character. They might well need, also, to be told to "love their neighbors *as them-selves;*" but at least it could be assumed that they initially loved themselves, which cannot be universally assumed among today's thinking people.

In reading the New Testament, therefore, we not only have to see what we find there, *and why;* we have also to notice WHAT IS TAKEN FOR GRANTED.

One passage which troubles some people in relation to Creative Visualization (although it deals with the subject of prayer, not of Creative Visualization) is in Matthew, Chapter 6, verses 7 and 8:

And when you are praying, do not use meaningless repetition, as the Gentiles do, for they suppose that

*they will be heard for their many words. Therefore do
not be like them; for your Father knows what you need,
before you ask Him.*

Matthew has another passage in the same chapter
(verses 25 to end) on the excellent theme of *Do not be
anxious,* which is sound counsel whether you are praying,
doing Creative Visualization, doing everything, anything
or nothing at all about your future. Whatever you decide
to do, you should BELIEVE IN IT, or until you can
believe you should *suspend judgment*: that is to say, you
should wait in a truly open-minded way to see what
comes. ANXIETY IS ENTIRELY DESTRUCTIVE, not
only of the delicate astral patterns but of you, your energy, sleep, digestion and nerves. That is why, although you
should prudently make up your mind to do *something*
about your future (and Creative Visualization is the best
form of mental work you can put in on it) still, to do
nothing at all would be BETTER THAN TO WORRY!

But to return to Matthew. His job was taking taxes
at a toll-gate (Chapter 9 verse 9) so perhaps he himself
did worry rather much about money; that could be why
he specially collected counsels on this subject. At any
rate, the people whose stories he tells in his Gospel are
very natural human beings, and when they want anything they ASK FOR IT in a perfectly natural way. The
Christ gives it to them, too; *without a word of rebuke
although they ask for "earthly" benefits,* usually
restored health for themselves or someone else.

Thus we have *the Leper* (Chapter 8 verse 2):— *Lord, if You are willing You can make me clean.* We have *the Centurion* (Chapter 8 verse 6):— *Sir, my servant is lying paralyzed at home* ... And we have *the Ruler* (Chapter 9 verse 18):— *My daughter has just died: but come and lay Your hand on her, and she will live.*

Were these stories told *to turn people away from* seeking a high remedy for their earthly sorrows? Or who could have expected these people to refrain from asking for those benefits?

If we look at the other Gospels, we even find people *being prompted by the Christ to state explicitly what they wanted*, even though their needs were evident. Thus we are told the story of *Blind Bartimaeus* (Mark chapter 10 verses 46 through 52):— *"What do you want Me to do for you?" Jesus asked him. "Master, I want to see again," the blind man told Him.* Similarly we have *the sick man by the Pool of Bethsaida* (John chapter 5 verse 6):— *When Jesus saw him lying there, and knew that he had already been a long time in that condition, He said to him, "Do you wish to get well?"*

Surely from these instances we should learn that it is good for people, and has from ancient times been KNOWN to be good for people, *TO STATE EXPLICITLY WHAT THEY DESIRE!*

But we have more New Testament texts to note.

There is the outstanding statement (Mark chapter 11 verses 22 through 24):— *"Have faith in God. Truly I say to you, whoever says to this mountain, 'Be taken up and cast into the sea,' and does not doubt in his heart, but believes that what he says is going to happen; it shall be granted him. Therefore I say to you, all things for which you pray and ask, believe that you have received them, and they shall be granted you."* The next verse deals with forgiving others in prayer so as to receive forgiveness oneself, so this passage is probably connected with that in Matthew chapter 6 which leads up to the "Lord's Prayer," and which has the words *"Go into your inner room, and . . . pray to your Father who is in secret."*

NOT "your Father up there beyond the sky!" This God in whom the hearers are bidden to have faith is the same God referred to in Luke chapter 17 verse 21,

*"THE KINGDOM OF GOD IS WITHIN YOU"**

To read through the New Testament, taking in the full import of this page, should clarify many things.

---

*All the other quotations from the N.T. in this chapter are taken from *The New American Standard Bible*. This sentence is according to both the King James version and Charles B. Williams' *The New Testament in the Language of the People,* which in our opinion make the meaning on this point clearer. *The New American Standard Bible* has "the Kingdom of God is in your midst," which is substantially the same, but some people take it to refer simply to the physical presence of Jesus among the people he was then addressing. This does not work, because the statement immediately preceding it, "The kingdom of God cometh not with observation," (or, "is not coming with signs to be observed") would then have to ignore the miracles.

Finally we come to the passage which chiefly answers, and elucidates, that other passage (Matthew chapter 6 verses 7 and 8) with which we began this survey. The story now to be considered is generally known as *The Parable of the Importunate Widow* (Luke chapter 18 verses 1 through 8).

This lady had an enemy whom she feared, or against whom at any rate she felt the law ought to protect her. So she went to the judge of the city, who, for his part, *did not fear God, and did not respect man.* He was inclined to ignore the widow's complaint, and did nothing. So she came back to him, and complained again. And again. And again. At last, he, who feared nothing else, dreaded the continual coming of the widow, and granted what she sought.

And the Lord said, "Hear what the unrighteous judge said; now shall not God bring about justice for His elect, who cry to Him day and night, and will He delay long over them?"

Contrasting this with the passage in Matthew, we see that the hearers are in fact told *to say explicitly what they want,* and *to repeat the procedure until they get it.* As to the warning about *"meaningless repetition,"* this evidently is a plain warning against the repetition of words that are meaningless (or that don't say what YOU mean) even when first uttered.

So the New Testament really ADVOCATES spiritual and mental means of fulfilling your earthly needs.

There is however one more reservation which a number of people are inclined to feel with regard to using such means. To seek a needed article is acceptable to them; to seek to obtain *money* in this way is still "suspect." They react, indeed, as many of our ancestors must have reacted in remote times when barter was the established and respectable form of trade, and money was "new-fangled" and maybe displeasing to the Gods.

There undoubtedly was such a time in the past. There may very well be a time in the future when the use of money has no place in the prevailing culture. In this present time, however, and in this present culture, money is the accepted medium for obtaining what you need, whether you need your dinner or a seminar on meditation. Besides, there are some benefits which could be obtained by Creative Visualization, *but which a man would not be wise to seek unless he had some assured amount of money with which to maintain them or to keep them within his orbit:* a house, a car, a wife . . .

(This consideration comes into the subject of "building in steps" which we shall mention again.)

Money, then, is something which normally appeals to us at the mental rather than at the emotional level, although we can easily make it appeal to us at the emotional level, not so much for its own sake as for the sake of the things we mean to do with it. In order to avoid possible inner conflict, however, we may need to ensure that the idea of money is not (perhaps unconsciously) *repugnant* to our emotional nature: either as being "outside the natural order," or because of a rule in our childhood that money was "not polite to discuss," seeming thereby to be placed for some uncomprehended reason within the same category as bodily functions.

As a matter of fact, within the "body politic" of any organized nation or community of people, money has a definite function, too real to be considered as metaphorical; it involves the kind of highly accurate symbolism which truly fulfills the role it represents. Vitalizing, nourishing, providing the means of renewal and of different kinds of activity, providing means of material growth and of mental achievement, money represents *the blood,* and the health of the corporate whole depends upon its circulation.

Like the blood supply to a limb, money assures the individual person of the power to live and act at will in the community, so far as the one factor can assure this. A young man, becoming interested in the deeper things of life, was asked his occupation and at once apologized: "I'm an insurance salesman — retirement insurance, insurance to cover children's education, that sort of thing." It was pointed out to him that he had no cause to apologize. He was helping people to see and to act upon the importance of *guaranteeing the life-sustaining flow* to those retiring people, to those children, so that they could continue to function in their rightful ways.

One of the chief errors with regard to money is to withhold it from good use, to hoard it. (This of course is a different thing from saving up for some special use.)

With "low-level" gains there is not usually much danger: money earned by work in the material world is largely not "gain" but "exchange," while anything gained by merely astral activity, as we have said, is usually transitory. With gains activated from a high level, however (*the way which will be yours to employ as seems best to you, when you have read this book*), it is important to KEEP UP THE CIRCULATION.

Just as each part of your own body operates as part of the plan of your total living system, so you will be operating as *part of the plan of the Cosmos*. You would not preserve one of your arms in better health by putting a tourniquet on it to keep the blood supply in it. (Not unless the arm was very badly injured, and then only for a short time!) The arm would soon become permanently damaged. It would DIE.

So you, if you were to hoard your gains, would be putting yourself literally OUT OF CIRCULATION, making yourself no longer a part of the current of life. USE PRUDENTLY AND WELL whatever you attract to yourself, and (to repeat) KEEP UP THE CIRCULATION.

A large book could be written on the ethical use of money, but we need only look at these fundamental principles to see that in our culture, as it is now and as it has been developing for centuries, the misuse of money is (like that of any of the earth's resources) the misuse of *a thing which is good in itself*. If we need money to develop our own way of life, to express and evolve our own selfhood, we do right to seek this from higher sources. Indeed, John Wesley (1703-1791), a man of great spiritual insight as well as practical ability, when he was asked once what basic counsel he would give to his followers on the subject of money, replied briefly:

GET ALL YOU CAN. GIVE ALL YOU CAN.

Let us leave now the subject of money and think how, in fact, we could apply this same briefly-expressed principle to other manifestations of the life force, such as STRENGTH–HEALING; INNER VISION–EXPRESSION THROUGH THE ARTS; KNOWLEDGE–TEACHING; WISDOM–GUIDANCE. There are many ways and modes in which such giving can be done; but in all cases, so that you may be able to *continue the operation*, you will need:

TO MAINTAIN, AND DRAW FROM, YOUR OWN LINK WITH HIGHER SOURCES.

TO CONTINUE, IN ONE WAY OR ANOTHER, TO KEEP UP THE OUTWARD CIRCULATION.

Naturally, you do not have to adopt all the ways of giving that we have mentioned. You can "keep up the circulation" without doing any of them specifically. *Think how much good it does people if they just meet someone who goes around radiating vitality, confidence, optimism, friendliness!* The "someone" may be a doctor, a ticket-collector, a student — whoever — he or she can "make the day" for quite a lot of people. BUT ONLY IF THE VITALITY AND THE REST OF IT IS REALLY THERE TO GIVE!

When *you* have the life force flowing in plenty *your* way, that is the kind of person YOU will be. (And probably you will be much more, too.)

This plenty, this continual channeling of power from higher levels outward, will not only help in gaining your more easily imaged needs. Think of the general benefit it can bring to your mental life, your emotional life, your bodily life. Think of the benefit to your health, to your bodily tone.

Many people are so accustomed to being "not sick" that when they discover the great potential of Creative Visualization, it never even occurs to them that good health is one of their needs. So, at your Creative Visualization sessions (and at other times, too) give a deliberate moment to seeing yourself, experiencing your life, as HEALTHY, STRONG, CONFIDENT, POISED, ATTRACTIVE and RADIANT.

How is this done?

It can be done a dozen ways, but here is a tried and valuable way, which can form an integral part in your Creative Visualization program generally.

What do we mean by "higher levels?" Ultimately, you picture ONE higher level, from which everything else that comes to you emanates. Different people would give different names here, all with somewhat different connotations:

God

The Divine Flame within me

My Higher Self

My Divine Friend (or Lover)

My Guardian Angel

If you know something of Qabalah or Yoga or other Wisdom-teachings, you may have a favorite name or concept to bring in here. If you haven't or if you don't feel sure, the *Higher Self* is probably your safest choice.

Your Higher Self is not to be confused with your Lower Self, but equally, it is concerned *entirely with you.* It is truly a spark of the Divine Mind and is in perpetual harmony and unity with that Mind, but you need never be troubled by thoughts of its being too busy looking after all the millions of other people, or in scheduling the Galaxies, to look after *you.*

YOU AND YOUR DESTINY ARE UNIQUELY IMPORTANT. YOU ARE UNIQUELY IMPORTANT TO YOUR HIGHER SELF. SELF-DEVELOPMENT

IS NOT COMPETITIVE. YOUR ADVANCEMENT IS NOT CUTTING ANYONE ELSE OUT—JUST THE CONTRARY!

So now, WHERE is this high source? Or rather, since it is a spiritual reality and not a material one, *where shall we picture it to be?*

If you are talking about God, you are likely to say "up there." If you are talking about the Divine Flame, you are likely to say "in here." If you are talking about your Higher Self, you might say either. Either is true. And neither is really adequate, but "up there" and "in here" at least give you something you can picture!

Either way, stand erect with feet together, arms hanging free, and commence your Rhythmic Breath.

Picture intense white light, scintillating and pulsating, streaming out from some place deep within you — from within your psyche — flooding every part of you, physical and non-physical, and emanating from your total body surface, spreading around you so that you are surrounded in every direction by an elliptical shape of luminous and living whiteness.

OR,

See the source of this wonderful light as an effulgent white globe some way above your head. From this globe the scintillating and pulsating light comes down into, and permeates, every part of your physical and non-physical being, at the same time spreading around you so that you are surrounded in every direction by

Surrounded and permeated by the Light of the Higher Self

an elliptical shape of luminous and living whiteness.
EITHER WAY,

Experience this light not only as an intense and all-permeating radiance, but also as a pulsating warmth like that of powerful but beneficent sunshine. Peace, happiness and complete confidence saturate your psyche and surround you, even as the white light and powerful warmth saturate and surround you.

Although the light entirely surrounds and permeates you, you can concentrate attention upon this or that part. See it course, glittering, vitalizing, *through your physical body*. Feel it, cleansing and warming, as it penetrates a stiff shoulder or any other area which may be bothering you. (Keep up your Rhythmic Breath as you do this.) Feel its influence, at once tranquilizing and energizing, right through to the tips of your fingers and toes as well as in the depths of your psyche. After a while, when you feel quite peaceful in contemplating it, you can gently let it fade from awareness. Later in this book you will read how to combine the experience of filling yourself with the light of the Higher Self with the most powerful practices of Creative Visualization. Nevertheless, this present practice is and will remain of eminent importance in your life. This is a way you can FEEL AND KNOW just a little of the benevolence of your Higher Self towards you. EXPERIENCE IT AS FULLY AND AS OFTEN AS YOU CAN — DAILY OR MORE OFTEN — AND *KNOW* THAT YOU LIVE AND MOVE WITHIN IT!

Checkpoint

4

- Continue practicing Visualization as this has been developed (see Checkpoints, Chapter 3).

- Continue practicing Creative Relaxation.

- Take every opportunity to utilize the Rhythmic Breath.

- You may not *feel* aware of all the Four Levels of your existence, but you should work out, try to realize in your own terms, what each of them means in your life. *Repeat this endeavor from time to time, as your awareness of the four levels is likely to develop.*

- Experience the all-pervading Light of your Higher Self as described at the end of this chapter, choosing whichever of the two methods comes most naturally to you. "Keep up the circulation" by means of this experience DAILY (or more often) for your own benefit and for others!

• If the New Testament teachings are of personal importance to you, go through (particularly) the Four Gospels and the Acts of the Apostles; see how often people are invited to benefit in their material lives by means of Divine Power. *Make a note of your favorite texts.*

Study Points

5

Everything comes to you through the Higher Self.

1. The power of the Higher Self is channeled through the Conscious and Unconscious levels of your own psyche.

2. Action takes place on the corresponding levels of the external universe.

Do not specify a Source of Supply in the Material World for what you want:

1. Because the real source is at the Spiritual Level.

2. Because what appears to be the most obvious material source may not, in fact, be the right one.

Avoid cluttering your Emotional Nature with *False Wishes:*

1. False Wishes rob you of time, energy and attention — CONCENTRATION
2. False Wishes rob you of some part of your power of decision — RESOLUTION.
3. False Wishes rob you of PATIENCE.

Never offer a price in your Creative Visualization work!

1. Expect what you need from the Plenty of the Universe.
2. Any concept of "bargaining" for what you want limits your Creative Visualization work to a level below the Higher Self.
3. Be confident in knowing you will attain your wishes — any self-limitation (fear, anxiety, denial of self-worth) shuts the door upon the Higher Self.

Spiritual Abundance

5

Where does everything come from which you obtain by means of Creative Visualization?

So far as the material world is concerned, one thing comes from one source and another from another; but, for the purposes of your Creative Visualization activity, you need not be, and should not be, concerned with anything but the *spiritual* source of supply. And it will make your practice simpler, and therefore more effective, if you think of the Source of Supply as being that one which does indeed bring these various benefits into your ambience. There are, as we have indicated, various ways in which you can conceive of, and name, this Source. It has to designate the high Being with whom you personally have a direct and profound relationship.

Throughout the rest of this book, we shall for brevity refer to this simply as *the Higher Self.*

Whatever you decide is the immediate thing to visualize for, whether a material or a non-material objective, it is in full confidence to be visualized as coming to you from that spiritual source.

Truly, by *the power of this source channeled through the conscious and unconscious levels of your own psyche,* the action takes place on the corresponding levels of the external universe, to bring about the presentation to you on the earthly level of what you have imaged. *That is WHY you can truly affirm that what you visualize IS YOURS NOW.*

Astrally it is YOURS, because you have implanted it in astral reality; mentally and spiritually it is YOURS, because you are activating those levels by means of your own mental and spiritual forces so that what you create astrally shall be REALIZED materially.

In the next chapter you will see how to carry out this operation with greater exactitude. At present it is good to consider some *mistakes you should avoid.*

If you have read any other works on Creative Visualization, whether old books or more recent, you will have noticed that there is almost always a warning against specifying or visualizing a source of supply in the material world for what you want; but scarcely ever are you given a REASON for this warning. There are in fact *two* reasons for it, BOTH VERY IMPORTANT.

The first reason why you should not specify or visualize a material source of supply for what you are seeking, is that by so doing you could easily obscure your perception of, or even your faith in, THE SPIRITUAL SOURCE OF SUPPLY. *The second reason* is, that what seems to you the most obvious material source of supply MAY NOT IN FACT BE THE RIGHT ONE, and so you might be causing delay and wasting effort by "barking up the wrong tree."

Some years back, in London, England, a self-taught scholar was delving into his own line of research in traditional Alchemy, a difficult subject in any circumstances. He had found a vital clue which pointed to the writings of one of the less understood medieval philosophers, but, though he searched carefully through his own collection of books and through the catalogs of many public libraries, he could find no means to pursue this line any further. In fact, every librarian he spoke to on the subject stared at him as at someone who had just stepped from Noah's Ark. He resolved to try Creative Visualization.

What he really needed was a quantity of INFORMATION on the medieval philosopher (whom we can call "Doctor Susconditus"). *What he asked for*, by sheer habit of mind, was A BOOK on the teachings of Doctor Susconditus. Now, books are often excellent things, but there are books and books; and sometimes a subject is better approached in other ways.

A few weeks after he had begun his practice of Creative Visualization, one of the librarians he had contacted sent him a circular from a European publisher, announcing an offset edition from an early folio of one of the Doctor's major works. Our friend took this leaflet to a bookstore, where a clerk worked out how much a copy would cost him. It would be very expensive, and he would have to pay in advance; nevertheless, he decided to place an order.

When the book arrived some months later, to his dismay he found it was so much reduced in size from the original as to be practically illegible anyway, aside from the fact that Doctor Susconditus' Latin, notorious even among medievalists, was very different from the classical Latin of our friend's schooldays. In fact, he had wasted both time and money to no purpose.

One thing seemed clear, however: his Creative Visualization had certainly worked. He began again, with a different pronouncement: "I want to learn of the teachings of Doctor Susconditus!"

The next weekend, taking a walk by the river in the early morning as he enjoyed doing, he got into conversation with a young man who seemed to be casually admiring the rather chilly view. To the surprise of both, they soon became engrossed in discussing the arcane interests they evidently shared. Soon, over breakfast at an early-opening cafe, it transpired that the stranger's home was far from London and, having accidentally gotten himself stranded, he hadn't a clue what to do about it. He had, in fact, panicked. Our friend, however, having learned in a harder school, soon pointed out that a collect-call to the young man's father, and his own hospitality until the father's arrival or monetary response, would easily solve the whole problem. Gratefully the young stranger replied, "If ever there is anything I can do for you . . ."

Whereupon our friend heard his own voice saying spontaneously, *"What I want is to learn of the teachings of Doctor Susconditus!"*

Now he was not looked at as if he had just stepped from Noah's Ark. "Why, yes," replied the other, "I know the very man to help you: probably the greatest living authority on Doctor Susconditus in the English-speaking world. He's an old schoolmaster of mine. He's very shy of being interviewed, hates publicity, but if I write to him he probably will see you."

So it was arranged; and our friend not only gained the immediate knowledge he needed. He gained the benefit of a university man's trained understanding of how to organize knowledge and, too, (because the old schoolmaster was delighted to encounter another mind's fresh approach to his own favorite subject) an insight into the great enmeshings of alchemical thought with other fields of study. (Oh, and he donated the offset volume to the old master's college. They were very happy to have it in their library catalog, even if nobody could read it!)

So (a) specify exactly what you want, but also (b) DON'T specify a material source of supply. There is more than that, however, to be learned from this story. As with so many of these real-life stories about success- ful Creative Visualization (and a tremendous number could be told) you can notice an almost "legendary" quality about the narrative. It makes no difference whether we are dealing with characters from centuries back or present-day people, it makes no difference what may be their age or sex or walk in life, they all seem to have been caught up for the time being into a world of golden light and of rightness of speech and action. *Yet they are true stories.* You may, yourself, have experi- enced moments in life when you have consciously known you "couldn't put a foot wrong."

This is characteristic of a link-up between your rational mind and the *archetypal level* of existence, which means that you are indeed "acting with power," the power channeled down from the Higher Self. Some- times, of course, this can happen when you are not at all aware of it, at least not until you look back afterwards upon the episode. But when you are aware of it, it is very enlightening.

When once you know, and are sure of, the feeling of this direct link with the Higher Self in archetypal action (as if you were living through the working-out in reality of some ancient myth) *you are not likely to fall into the other errors which are to be described here.*

Furthermore, even without your having gained this awareness when you are visualizing for something, you will be much helped and strengthened by
RESOLUTION
CONCENTRATION
PATIENCE
aided by Rhythmic Breathing and Creative Relaxation.

For one of the faults to avoid — we have mentioned it before — is the confusion of *nervous tension* with *emotional intensity*. Not only is nervous tension destructive of the qualities mentioned above, it is an implicit denial (if you consider it) of that *belief in success* which is a part of effective Creative Visualization. You KNOW you are building up, astrally, and are infusing with spiritual reality, that which is to come to you in the material world. *Tension is the natural prelude to action* — but you ARE ALREADY taking the action which is to be effective in this case, so what need for tension? Desire strongly, *but not with your nerves!*

Built-up, prolonged tension is a sign of fear, of frustration, of anxiety. Breathe rhythmically, relax, smile: BANISH TENSION!

Another fault against which you should be very much on guard is that of allowing your emotional nature to become *cluttered with false wishes*. It can easily happen, in these days when not only continual advertising but also "public opinion" (usually an equally artificial product) tries to decree what you like, what you want.

This does not mean that you should ignore advertisements altogether. A sensible study of them will teach us what is to be had in the world, what we can seek in the world and what the world (including our fellow-humans) may expect of us. They are educationally useful, not only for young people but also for older people who are sometimes inclined to forget or deliberately ignore the fact that standards and availabilities of all kinds change continually. Advertisements are an important part of the world's news.

Good advice, too, is not to be ignored. You may have settled in your mind that you want (say) a house and a car; but which first? And of what kind, and where, and when? These are questions on which other people's opinions besides your own wishes may be well worth knowing.

What you have to avoid is being like the woman who goes to a sale for a coat, and comes back with ten dresses instead, all "bargains," but five of which don't fit her and the rest she doesn't like. We are here referring, of course, not only to buying *things,* but much more to "buying" desires, letting suggestions and wishes be foisted on you when they are not yours AND YOU DON'T WANT THEM.

These false wishes and daydreams DO cost you something, and it is something valuable to you. They cost you time, energy, attention — *concentration* — and some part of your power of decision — *resolution! Qualities you need for your Creative Visualization.*

So ALWAYS see yourself as *happy, prosperous, tranquil, healthy and socially successful,* but ONLY give detailed attention to those aspects of the picture which you feel ought to have it at this present time. And FREQUENTLY call to mind the existence of *your spiritual source of supply!*

A crisis situation can be very effective in leading us to cut out "clutter" and to identify, and act for, the next requisite object to pull us out of the crisis; but, too, *it is precisely in a crisis situation that anxiety, doubt, tension have most to be guarded against.* The story of Annie Z. may be a helpful example here.

(Noticeably, most of our stories of Creative Visualization come from people in rather underprivileged walks of life. This is NOT BY ANY MEANS a sign that it can't be used by, or won't work for, people who are already in a secure and prosperous position. Frequently, the things that people in secure and prosperous positions want are not readily purchasable:— a man has a rare antique jar, lacking only the lid; a girl has a nervous condition which the most expensive specialists have failed to cure; the manufacturer of a chemical product seeks a good use for a waste substance. Such people can, and in many instances do, use Creative Visualization successfully, the conditions for success being just the same for them as for other people. But their success does not stand out so strikingly; again, MANY SUCCESSFUL MEN USE CREATIVE VISUALIZATION ALL THE TIME, BUT KEEP THEIR SUCCESSES AS THEIR OWN PERSONAL "SECRET."

This they are entitled to do, and when we come to know of such facts we are not entitled to publish them.)

So we return to the "underprivileged," although nobody who met Annie Z. would have guessed it, AND SHE PERSONALLY NEVER THOUGHT OF HERSELF IN THAT WAY. For a number of years, indeed, she lived the life of a cultivated, well-leisured single girl, and the main difference between her and her friends was that they wouldn't have dared disturb their investments, and she didn't possess any to disturb. *But this again had no place in her thoughts:* "I HAVE ALL THE GOLD IN THE SUN," she said, and visualized everything she needed coming to her from that radiant source.

(YES, OF COURSE IT WORKED!)

If she had one fault in her visualization technique, it was *diffuseness of purpose.* The effects were continual, startling, but of course correspondingly small, though they all contributed to her life-style. Then one day she learned that *she was going to lose her apartment,* because the old building in which it was situated was due for demolition.

She kept her head: "all the gold in the Sun" was not going to fail her now. Temporarily she stopped her Creative Visualization "sidelines:" the complimentary theater tickets, the stylish hair-dos for which she sometimes modeled, the offcuts of exclusive fabrics, and the rest. She visualized herself in an apartment rather like her existing one, save in one respect which she meant to change. The old building had no elevator; she did not mind its age, but she was heartily sick of the stairs. She was willing enough to live on the first floor, so she pictured a first-floor apartment, and sun-rays with hands rather like those on the Aten-disc in Egyptian paintings giving it to her. She also pictured herself decorating the apartment as she would like it, *because to do something which at once marks an article as one's own is a most powerful way of laying claim to it.*

A couple of weeks after she embarked on this program, she was talking to a friend who mentioned that a nephew of her husband's was coming from overseas as a student, and the husband was keeping for him a first-floor apartment which had become vacant in some property they owned; the boy could have it in return for re-decorating it and taking turns with tending the boiler. Annie knew instantly that this was the kind of break she was looking for, but, realizing there is Plenty in the world for all, she made no attempt to take over the young student's good luck.

Another week, however, and the friend's husband contacted Annie to ask if she would be interested in the apartment on the same terms. The nephew had taken one look at the big, old-fashioned rooms with their chipped and faded paintwork, and had opted at once to go and live in a regular students' hostel and to have the company of boys his own age.

This brings us to the next subject on which a warning should be given.

It is *quite all right* if, when something for which you have been doing Creative Visualization comes your way, you find you have to pay for it some price you can well afford, whether in money or in work. If MORE is asked than you can conveniently give, just ignore the offer and go on with your visualization program: this first manifestation of a response is NOT THE ONE FOR YOU. If you visualized for a piano, for instance, you may find that old pianos, new pianos, pianos that would cost you thousands of dollars and given-for-free pianos with no wires left in them, all may be brought to your notice both before and after THE RIGHT ONE. That's the way it goes. You may be offered an acceptable gift, or you may decide to pay a reasonable price for a reasonable article. *Both are O.K., and the choice is your affair.*

What you should NEVER do is to offer a price, whether in money, goods or work, IN YOUR CREATIVE VISUALIZATION ACTIVITIES. Your rational mind must keep control while allowing the unconscious levels to act on your behalf; and to try to make pacts or bargains with the unconscious levels is to give up a part of that control. EXPECT WHAT YOU NEED FROM THE PLENTY OF THE UNIVERSE.

WHAT YOU WANT TO GIVE, GIVE FREELY AND "CUT THE STRINGS." Only that way you need have no regrets.

Above all, when you have entered upon any Inner Development program (and Creative Visualization is a form of Inner Development, the development and use of your hidden faculties) you should NEVER, even in casual conversation, say the kind of foolish thing which we sometimes hear, "I'd give ANYTHING if only . . ." Such a desire to bargain can only arise from fear, the fear that what one dearly wants may not come to pass unless something is offered in exchange; but this impulse is deceptive.

By making an attempt of this kind, one is putting oneself in a WEAK position, not a strong one. The only STRONG position is that of total confidence, that without fee and without compromise, the thing one wants WILL COME TO PASS because one has clearly imaged it, and because one infuses that image WITH THE POWER OF THE HIGHER SELF.

One of the barriers which a lot of people put up against themselves is the barrier of "conscience." They make an objection, either knowingly or unknowingly, that they shouldn't have this or that because they have done nothing to deserve it; or, worse still, they think they ought not to have it because of some past error or fault of theirs. They assume they ought to deprive themselves, punish themselves.

This idea of some duty of self-punishment is altogether contrary to the spiritual truth of the matter. YOUR HIGHER SELF DOES NOT INQUIRE WHAT YOU DESERVE!

The concepts of reward and punishment are very convenient and, usually, effective ways of regulating human conduct in the material world. Domestic animals can to some extent be conditioned to respond to them also. *But they go no higher than that.* You are quite right to have a "conscience;" but it is part of your Lower Self, not of your Higher Self. It is conditioned to a great extent by what you were taught in childhood, and also by your personal experiences and observations in the world.

That is the reason why so many people's consciences tell them so many different things. Your conscience is *not* "the voice of God," and you should certainly never think it has any right to punish you. The REAL "voice of God" in you — the Divine Flame which is your Higher Self — is that which will raise you up as far as you will let yourself be raised, lavish love upon you as far as you are willing to receive it. UNCONDITIONALLY.

If you have somehow wronged another person you should certainly make restitution to that person, whether by material or spiritual means according to circumstances. BUT WHAT YOU DO SHOULD BE DONE ENTIRELY FOR THAT PERSON'S BENEFIT. NOT TO DEPRIVE YOURSELF OF SOMETHING.

TWO WRONGS DON'T MAKE A RIGHT.
LOVE YOURSELF, FORGIVE YOURSELF, LET YOURSELF GO FREE!

In an Outer Order document (written to guide junior members of the Order of the Sacred Word) published in

Volume I of *The Magical Philosophy*, is a general state-ment on self-criticism which may be helpful here:—

"We should never despond over ourselves; particu-larly with such words as 'I am proud, I am lazy, I am dishonest.' The essence and life of the soul is in action and motion, not in any static condition. The same is true of the so-called virtues. If it has been judged of a man that he is just, that is of no avail if he acts unjustly today; but if he has acted unjustly today, let him redress it by acting justly tomorrow. And thought is action, upon its own more subtle level: it often is more powerful than outward action."

Self-limitation shuts the door upon the Higher Self. It is, besides, a shocking travesty of Christianity, a religion whose initial purpose was avowedly to release people from false restrictions. But we have said something of Christianity's true teachings in Chapter 4.

None of us can claim to be entirely WITHOUT FEAR all the time, particularly when something which matters a great deal is still not manifest on the material level of existence. We are human, and it is not to be expected that we should live in that way. If a fear can, however, be suspended *for the duration of our Creative Visualization,* as it should be, we are likely to find our renewed confidence will last much longer. Here we have several great helps; there is not only Rhythmic Breath-ing and Creative Relaxation, we should remember to use also the *Power of Song.*

Sing in your heart at least, sing the tune or even the words also aloud if that is possible; not for others to analyze, but TO TELL YOURSELF WHAT YOU KNOW. Song is something which the unconscious levels understand, *because its appeal is emotional;* so in that way you can get through to them.

King Alfred (848-900) was called "the Great" for more things than being a king and fighting the Danes. He had some correspondence with the Patriarch of Jerusalem, he may have sent a mission to India, he translated various didactic works from Latin into the English of his day, and he compiled two books (one of which survives) of sayings and writings that particularly appealed to him. So scholarly a man was certainly not through lack of imagination the brave warrior that he was. One of his secrets of courage has come down to us, and is thus put into the speech of our day:

IF YOU HAVE A FEARFUL THOUGHT,
TO A WEAKLING TELL IT NOT:
TO YOUR SADDLE-POMMEL BREATHE IT,
    AND RIDE FORTH SINGING!

Checkpoint

5

- Continue with your basic practices in Visualization, Relaxation and Rhythmic Breathing.

- Experience the all-pervading Light of your Higher Self, and KEEP UP THE CIRCULATION!

- Don't define a material source of supply for what you plan to gain by Creative Visualization: BE INTENSELY AWARE OF THE SPIRITUAL SOURCE!

- Don't cultivate nervous tension (destructive) in place of emotional intensity (creative). BREATHE RHYTHMICALLY. RELAX, SMILE!

- Don't cultivate false wishes: KEEP CLEARLY IN MIND WHAT YOUR TRUE GOALS ARE!

- Don't bargain with the invisible world — RECEIVE FREELY, AND GIVE FREELY.

- Never think of any deprivation as a punishment. THE HIGHER SELF ONLY LOVES AND GIVES!

- If any doubts or fears trouble you, don't allow them more reality than you must. KEEP QUIET ABOUT THEM: SING OF YOUR HOPES!

Study Points

6

Creative Visualization allows you to PLAN YOUR LIFE!
1. The fulfillment of each specific need should carry you a step further towards the attainment of your real goals.
2. "Stairway" plans make attainment of your goals easier.
3. Such Stairway plans also make it easier to attain the "extras" without upsetting the main line of progress mapped by the Stairway.

The Foundation Work of every Creative Visualization project reviewed:
1. Daydream — many times.
    See yourself enjoying what you are going to attain.

2. Creative Relaxation — vital to healthy life. *Counteract any anxiety which may be felt at the start of a project.*

3. Rhythmic Breathing — this should become part of your normal life pattern. *Work with that rhythm.*

4. Simple Creative Visualization Method (see Chapter 3): *Include this at the start of each new project. It will be superseded by Charging (see below).*

5. Sing about your objective.

6. Experience the LIGHT of your Higher Self (see Chapter 4).

The CHARGING technique:

1. Sit with erect spine in a balanced posture.

2. Relax.

3. Breathe Rhythmically.

4. Visualize your objective as contained within a White Circle.

5. Fill yourself with the Light of the Higher Self.

6. See visualized object glowing with the Light as your own radiance diminishes.

7. Charge it with words.

8. Let the charged image fade away from your vision.

The Master Method of Creative Visualization combines Foundation Work with the Charging Technique.

The Master Method can be further augmented with such techniques as:

1. Candle burning
2. Planetary Sphere Working

as procedures for linking with the lower levels of the psyche.

The Charging Technique can be used in combination with simple Divinatory Techniques in a reverse manner, to produce a desired condition.

The Stairway of Success

6

Besides the great benefits you gain directly from Creative Visualization, it brings you other benefits also as "side effects." (That is typical of any true form of inner development; when this is rightly pursued, as in the ways we show you, you go forward not merely in this or that faculty but AS A WHOLE BEING.)

One of the "side benefits" which is to be gained by using Creative Visualization is AN OPPORTUNITY TO PLAN YOUR LIFE CONSTRUCTIVELY, FOR WHAT *YOU* WANT.

Just as every day's Creative Visualization will build towards the fulfillment for you of some specific need, so the fulfillment of EACH SPECIFIC NEED in its turn should carry you a stage further towards the attainment of your REAL goals.

You may not be able to plan more than a step or so ahead at any given time, and it is better that your plans should remain flexible to your inner and outer development; but *the fact that you are in a position to plan as you go on* is what will make this structure raised by Creative Visualization distinctively YOURS.

Considered in this way, it is rather like building a stairway; each individual stair is built up of blocks, but each completed stair in turn lifts you one stage UP and ONWARD towards your main purpose.

As examples, let us take two men's variations on the familiar "house and car" pattern:

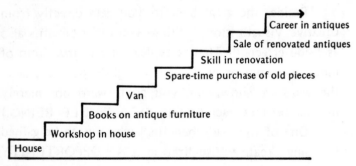

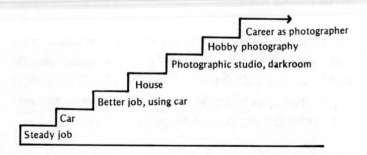

The Stairway

This does not mean that all your Creative Visualization programs have to be plainly utilitarian. The sample plans we have shown look very severe and practical because we have only shown their essential framework: the parts which link up, one with another, in a progressive unity. We have not shown where the first man visualized for, and got, the boat he wanted for his boys, nor have we put in the second man's home movie projector. It is EASIER for you to acquire such things, without upsetting your main line of progress, WHEN YOU HAVE COME SOME WAY with Creative Visualization, than by setting up a "separate current" for them during the earlier stages of your practice.

Whatever you may at the moment be visualizing for, you can use the objective upon your "top step" — or a symbol which will represent that objective to you — to typify your whole "stairway" and to keep that objective in mind. This will also help you make firm decisions if alternative ways of ascent make their appearance; DON'T be a slave to the exact plan you have made; *other ways up may prove to be better or quicker*, but DO assure yourself that the new path can take you where you want!

The point we are chiefly concerned to make here is that when there is a progressive "stairway" relationship among the MAIN ITEMS in a series of Creative Visualization programs, the earlier "steps" in the "stairway" DO REALLY MAKE IT EASIER FOR YOU to achieve, in due course, the later and higher steps.

This STEPPING-UP OF ACHIEVEMENT is so well known that it has become proverbial. There is the saying,

NOTHING SUCCEEDS LIKE SUCCESS.

There is also the *Parable of the Talents* in Matthew Chapter 25, verses 14 through 30, with its "negative aspect" relentlessly stated in verse 29:— *"For unto every one that hath shall be given, and he shall have abundance; but from him that hath not shall be taken away even that which he hath."* (It must always be remembered that harsh biblical statements like this one, or like the Old Testament utterance that "the sins of the fathers shall be visited upon the children," are NOT to be taken as *Divine decrees:* they are simply very shrewd observations on the way life usually is, and on that level nobody can deny them. But they CAN be "lived down," with resolution and with *insight into how they work.*)

The two reasons we have given for the intensification of success in Creative Visualization can be analyzed further. You should especially note the following:—

(1) Your confidence in your Creative Visualization increases as soon as you experience *real gain* from it. Your imagination and unconscious levels will correspondingly become *purged* of any old failure images.

(2) Thus you will become very COURAGEOUS, and also

more GENEROUS: generous not only in *giving,* but also in *hoping,* in *imagining,* in *judging,* in every aspect of your inner life. You may not at once see how, but it is a fact that limited hopes, narrow views, mean judgments, arise from *fears.* So COME OUT OF YOUR SHELL INTO THE FULL LIGHT OF DAY!

(3) Your Confidence of Success *radiates* in a way which affects other people. *So long as you don't try to explain it to them,* and *so long as you don't make them feel jealous or resentful,* THEY WILL LOVE HELPING YOU TO EVEN MORE SUCCESS.

YOUR SUCCESS IS THEIR DAYDREAM

and so, without even knowing about it, a lot of people will Creatively-Visualize MORE success for you!

Everybody loves a "success story" — so long as they can see the hero's (or heroine's) success as in any way THEIR success!

(4) In this, people are QUITE RIGHT. You ARE helping them! — in the same way that people always have been helped by the old stories, the youngest son who ended up as the luckiest one of the family, the girl who left the cinders and married a prince, all the myths and legends and fairy-tales — only it helps people a lot more when they see that such things happen IN REAL LIFE.

Thus, when these people see the Plenty of the Universe flowing from the archetypal level for *you*, and they feel they can *identify with you*, they are unconsciously being prepared — they are learning — to *expect the same plenty for themselves!* So they too, whether they understand it or not, *will begin Creative Visualization for themselves in the RIGHT way*. (You may remember how, right at the beginning of this book, we showed how all kinds of people do Creative Visualization, consciously or unconsciously, some in the RIGHT way — visualizing what they DESIRE — and other people in the WRONG way because they build up images of just what they DON'T want, what they FEAR.)

(5) Helping these particular people towards the right kind of Creative Visualization is a very good thing, but EVEN THAT ISN'T ALL THE GOOD YOU ARE DOING.

These people in their turn, as they come to experience the free flowing of the Plenty of the Universe, will open up in their life-attitudes, will become in different ways *more generous*, will SPREAD the circulation of material and of spiritual benefits *further than you alone ever could!* (And — remember again — spiritual and material benefits are all FORMS OF ENERGY.) So there is MORE LIFE, BETTER LIFE, FOR EVERYONE INCLUDING YOU!

But it is time now to come back to some aspects of Creative Visualization which you need to be able to deal with in a very exact and practical way.

Supposing you have an actual project in Creative Visualization, and have worked with it through the chapters of this book to this present point. If you are a beginner, you should have taken each step as it has been given; but if you have already completed a Creative Visualization project and want to start again with a new objective, you may wonder how much material you need from the earlier chapters. In any case, we have at this point to consider the ongoing necessity or otherwise for the earlier material.

(a) *Every new Creative Visualization project should begin with the "daydream" stage.* No matter how experienced you may be, don't rush or skimp this early nurturing of the project and the building-up of your emotional motivations. See yourself ENJOYING what you are going to gain by visualization. Do your day-dreaming last thing at night, after lunch, in a warm bath, any way you please but make it REAL, even if this is your ninety-ninth successful visualization!

(b) *The Creative Plan of Relaxation* is there to help you. Later in this book there are some programs based on it; unless and until you decide upon one of these, the frequency of your Creative Relaxation is entirely your choice. It is highly recommended, however, to counter-act the anxiety often felt in the early stages of a Creative Visualization project.

(c) We probably have said enough about *Rhythmic Breath* to show that the continued use of this should not depend upon your use of one program or another, but this valuable technique will in any case be needed for your future progress in Creative Visualization.

(d) The *simple Creative Visualization* method given in Chapter 3 is one of the stages through which you should bring every new Creative Visualization project. It will always be superseded when you begin the Charging Technique which is about to be given in this chapter. But (like the "daydream stage" also) there is no reason why you should not from time to time indulge in this as a morale-booster or if one day you want to put in a little extra activity.

(e) *Singing about your objective* can be done all the time or any time, from beginning to end of the program. It is good for the project and good for you, too, to sing, croon, chant, hum, murmur or mentally utter the secret song of your desire whenever opportunity offers. The only reason why we don't tell you to do this until Chapter 3 is because so many other things have to go into Chapters 1 and 2.

(f) *Experiencing the Light of your Higher Self* is strictly needed by beginners as a preliminary to the Charging Technique which follows. It is contained within that technique. We do not however say that the experience as a separate practice is thenceforward "not needed;" you can and should enjoy it for inner peace and renewal at any time. IT IS PART OF YOUR LIFE!

(The paragraphs (a) through (f) above comprise the practices which make up what will from now onward be called "The Foundation Work.")

The Charging Technique

You have nurtured your Creative Visualization objective from the first imaginings to clear-cut form and purpose. Now the project is to become a step in your STAIRWAY OF SUCCESS, whether for business, health or pleasure; whatever you intend.

You sit with spine erect, feet side by side, hands on thighs. You close your eyes.

You relax, keeping, however, the erect spine and the balanced posture.

You commence, and maintain, Rhythmic Breathing.

You visualize your objective.

Now you want to be certain to infuse this visualized objective with the power of your Higher Self. THIS IS MOST IMPORTANT FOR REAL AND DURABLE EFFECTS IN THE MATERIAL WORLD. So:—

(a) You visualize your objective as being *contained in a white circle.* (Not a very bright or shining circle, just white like chalk or paint, but COMPLETELY containing the visualized objective, whether this be a single thing, or a combination of things, or a scene, or a picture of yourself or of some other person.)

(b) You now fill yourself with the Light of your Higher Self, in the way you have chosen from the two methods given in the last pages of Chapter 4. Experience this as white light and glowing warmth throughout and around you. It may not at first be easy to do this without "losing" your visualized image in the circle, but THE MORE ATTENTION YOU HAVE GIVEN TO FILLING YOURSELF WITH THE LIGHT, the more easily you should succeed now. *You don't have to "look at" the Light filling you in order to be aware of it, any more than you have to look and check up when someone switches the light on in the room where you are.*

Having filled yourself with the Light of your Higher Self, *you have to transfer this light to your visualized object.* To do this, begin by "drawing back from" your visualized image, to make a slight distance between it and yourself, leaving it hanging in the air so to speak. This drawing back can at first be a slight physical movement; soon you will be accustomed to doing that in imagination also. See the visualized object becoming brighter and brighter, while you become less and less aware of the radiance in yourself. The image, still distinctly visualized, becomes glowing with the pulsating light, *but the radiance does not pass beyond the boundary of the white circle you have visualized around it.* You are charging the one image that you have formulated for the purpose, and nothing else. *Say meanwhile:*

WITH THE LIGHT OF MY HIGHER SELF I CHARGE THIS IMAGE, THAT IT BE REALIZED FOR ME IN THE MATERIAL WORLD.

Keep the light-filled image, in its circle, in visualization for a short time. (A few Rhythmic Breaths suffice for an "inner" activity of this sort; only with experience do you find how effective is truly concentrated action.) *Then let it slowly fade.*

Keep up your Rhythmic Breathing for a while after this vanishing is complete, then gently return your awareness to the outer world.

THIS IS THE SUPREMELY POTENT WAY TO BRING REALITY TO WHAT YOU VISUALIZE. Take time to consider this.

What we have told you is:—
To fill yourself with the Light of your Higher Self. To energize with this light your visualized and encircled Objective.

This has been for ages, both in the East and in the West, a major SECRET which has been carefully guarded in a succession of cults, and which, even to their faithful, has been given forth *only in veiled language.* Such secrets have often been called *"magico-religious."* We prefer to call them simply PSYCHOSOPHICAL, because they derive from a deep understanding of the psyche and the wisdom of its inherent nature.

Throughout the centuries, people have been fascinated by reports from different parts of the world (sometimes exaggerated, but sometimes quite literally true) of the deeds of certain wonder-workers who proclaim "IN THE NAME OF . . ." and marvels come to pass. Many people (including learned students of the Qabalah, who should have known better) have spent years, lifetimes, trying to find *the right Name* whose utterance would bring them this power. Of course, "In the Name of . . ." is only a cover-phrase whose true meaning is "IN THE POWER OF . . ." and the "right Name" is whatever is THE RIGHT NAME FOR *YOU* TO USE, FOR "THAT" WHOSE LIGHT MUST FILL YOU, the Higher Self, the Divine Flame Within.

THIS IS THE MOUNTAIN-MOVER!

When you become truly proficient in this method of Creative Visualization, there is literally NOTHING that can withstand you.

Consider Luke chapter 11 verses 34-36:—

"The light of the body is the eye: therefore when thine eye is single, thy whole body also is full of light; but when thine eye is evil, the body also is full of darkness . . . If thy whole body therefore be full of light, having no part dark, the whole shall be light, as when the bright shining of a candle doth give thee light."

Consider also these words of Pey of Mylapore (Madras), one of the medieval musician-saints whose hymns are still in popular use among present-day Hindus:—

"Lighting in my heart the bright lamp of knowledge, I sought and captured Him: softly THE LORD OF MIRACLES entered my heart and stayed there without leaving."

Consider also Dr. O. Carl Simonton, in the remarkable article by him and Stephanie Matthews-Simonton in the *Journal of Transpersonal Psychology* #1 (1975), "Belief Systems and Management of Emotional Aspects of Malignancy":—

"I have not found any patient [who showed spontaneous remission of cancer symptoms, or unexpectedly good responses] *that did not go through a similar visualizing process. It might be a spiritual process. God healing them, up and down the whole spectrum. But the important thing was WHAT THEY PICTURED AND THE WAY THEY SAW THINGS. THEY WERE POSITIVE, REGARDLESS OF THE SOURCE, AND THEIR PICTURE WAS VERY POSITIVE."*

Bearing in mind what we have already said of the Light with which the visualized image is to be charged, that it is "Power and Life-force and Love and Blessing all in one," it can be seen that a person ignorant of the technique as such, *but visualizing in a way which strongly infuses the created image with one of these modalities of the Light,* can succeed in his or her endeavor. The following true history is given in Volume III of *The Magical Philosophy:*—

"A certain young man was, through his hobby of rock-climbing, a cause of considerable concern to his mother. She did not allow herself to become a prey to worry, however, until one night she had a particularly vivid and horrifying dream in which she saw him struggling to regain his balance upon a narrow ledge, from which he eventually fell. After awaking from this nightmare, the mother was haunted by the mental image; over and over she saw it in her imagination, but the most frightful aspect of the matter was her certainty that this dream was some kind of premonition of an impending physical occurrence. The next time the memory of her dream overwhelmed her, instead of trying to dispel it she accepted it, and with great courage passively watched in her imagination the preliminary happenings. Then, at the critical moment, she exerted all her will to change the climax: to visualize her son as regaining his balance and reaching safety.

"Every time the mental image came back to her, she made the effort to change it in this way, until she was completely successful and the horror faded.

"Then, some time later, her son returned from a holiday and told her of his narrow escape from what had nearly been a fatal accident. He had reached a ledge, just as she had seen in her dream; he had lost his balance through trusting to an insecure rock, and had believed himself to be irrevocably falling over the precipice; then, as he said, a powerful gust of wind had suddenly risen to meet him, GIVING HIM JUST THE HELP THAT HE NEEDED TO REGAIN MASTERY OF THE SITUATION."

Every earthly circumstance has its astral counterpart, which in some circumstances we can perceive in advance. This mother, with great (though unconscious) insight, first CHANGED the astral image by visually creating her own version of the happening, and then, by the powerful current of her love (that is, by a beam sent down from the power of Supernal Motherhood within the psyche) she GAVE STABILITY AND MATERIAL REALITY TO HER VISUALIZATION.

These various texts and examples should help you to grasp the essence of the matter. In your own practice with this all-important technique, do not fail —

To *visualize* clearly the proposed objective,

To *enclose* it within a visualized ring,

To *charge* it with the Light of your Higher Self; all this being encompassed within the framework of balanced posture, relaxation, and Rhythmic Breathing, as we have explained. *Even if you are allowing two or three sessions for Creative Visualization, work with the Charging Technique only once daily* but persevere in this until your objective is gained. Remember to keep up the "Foundation Work;" and, when your objective is gained, say a "Thank you" to your Higher Self.

TO BRING A CREATIVE VISUALIZATION PROJECT RIGHT THROUGH THE "FOUNDATION WORK," AND TO COMPLETE IT WITH THE CHARGING TECHNIQUE IS CALLED *THE MASTER METHOD OF CREATIVE VISUALIZATION.*

It is easy to adapt this Method to most purposes. You may for example wish to use it *for the healing of another person, who may not be physically within reach.*

"Distant Healing" is often a simple sending of an extra "charge" of energy, life-force, to the person intended, together with an affirmation of that person's well-being. This can be in any case very helpful in assisting the natural self-renewing powers of the person to function in freedom from the deficiencies and obstacles produced by weakness, shock, and negative suggestion. TO BE ABLE TO AID THIS SELF-RENEWING IS ALWAYS A WORTHWHILE AND JOYFUL ACTION.

"Distant Healing" can be done in various ways. Sometimes people who cannot visualize, or who are not aware of the technique, just set up their Rhythmic Breath, fill themselves with the Light of the Higher Self (by whatever name) and then *send* it, directed by the hands and fingers, in the topographical direction of the intended recipient. This can, indeed, be effective.

However, for exact, powerful and lasting results, your procedure should be, after setting up your Rhythmic Breath, to *formulate an image* of the person who is to benefit (visualizing him or her as fit, happy, smiling and youthful) and *place a circle around this image;* then *charge it with the Light of your Higher Self,* holding it steadily in the Power and Love and Blessing of the Light, and finally *send* it by an inner impulse in the direction of that person, keeping the posture and Rhythmic Breath until after the image has faded from visualization.

The main framework of this technique should be kept unchanged, but you can vary your action as need be.

If for this type of action you are employing a photo-graph of the recipient as an aid to visualization, DON'T FORGET TO CLOSE YOUR EYES when you come to the actual time for visualization: *it is your visualized image* which is to be charged, *not the photograph!*

If you are carrying out this procedure on behalf of a person who has a localized trouble (say an earache, or a broken leg) you may want to visualize particularly the part of the body where the trouble is. Be sure, however, TO SEE THAT PART OF THE BODY AS COMPLETE-LY HALE AND WHOLE, and change your image to THE WHOLE PERSON, WELL AND HAPPY before you conclude. (For a broken leg, you might suitably see the person running or walking; for deafness, enjoying music, or so forth.)

Even when the person is present in the room with you, this technique can have special value when an internal organ is involved. (Of course, unless you can also use clairvoyance, a basic knowledge of anatomy is desirable here.)

No matter what the purpose of your action, on your own behalf or that of another person, although THE ACTIVITY OF YOUR HIGHER SELF IS IN ITSELF PERFECT, *you have* (in this, as in all that you do) *to function as a complete entity*. Therefore, any means that you can use to bring your Lower Self fully into accord with the action of your Higher Self, *is a good thing*. There are various ways in which this can be done.

We must give mention in this category to the traditional methods of *disciplined living,* which in a long-term view of the matter have so very much to offer the man or woman who is resolved on making a lifetime program of developing the inner faculties. There is no question here of "penance" or of any "glorification of suffering," any more than these considerations figure in the life of an Olympics champion. An abstemious but well-balanced diet (preferably vegetarian), daily physical exercise, daily exercise of the faculties of the psyche, frequent contact with the world of nature, an avoidance of whatever is found by the person in question to diminish available energy or to be at odds with the individual sense of fitness or rightness, is the basis of such a regimen. Over a long period, it can work wonders even for those with no great initial aptitude.

For the man or woman who does not wish to take so "committed" an attitude, however — who regards the development of inner faculties simply as a part of all-round living, perhaps — there are shorter cuts to bringing the Lower Unconscious into line with an intended project of Creative Visualization: and particularly are these shorter cuts valid for those who have already developed some psychic perceptions or abilities.

The Master Method, that is the Charging Technique supported by good use of the "Foundation Work" as it has been given, contains in itself all that is needed for full effectiveness, for ANYONE who perseveres.

The suggestions which follow here, of ways in which the Charging Technique may be combined with other practices, are only means to help you by creating a situation to which your emotional and lower unconscious levels can more easily respond. *Those given on this page require the full Master Method;* that is, you need to do the Foundation Work in preparation for the Charging Technique.

If, for example, you have some favorite procedure you already use in order to create special psychic conditions (such as candle-burning or planetary sphere-working), some procedure which, you feel, has already made a real link with the deeper levels of your psyche, this is something which *in a special way* you can use in connection with the Master Method of Creative Visualization. You will not be trying to guide your Higher Self or to supplement its power; these procedures work by means of associated ideas and emotions entirely upon the lower and deeper levels; you will be using a "language" which those levels already understand.

If you are accustomed (as an instance) to candle-burning, you can during your Charging Technique sessions burn the candles suited to the kind of result you intend: prosperity, love, or so forth. If you are accustomed to planetary work, you can employ the suitable color, incense etc., for whichever of the Spheres is appropriate to your purpose: Mercury for travel, Mars for justice, Jupiter for plenty, and so on.

If you are well accustomed to a divinatory procedure, then (when you are experienced in the Charging Technique also) there is an extremely interesting type of action which you can perform, *even without building up the "Foundation Work" for this operation specifically.* (Speedy action is sometimes desirable!) SO POWERFUL IS THIS MODE OF PROCEEDING, HOWEVER, THAT YOU ARE CAUTIONED TO BE VERY SURE BEFORE USING IT THAT THE DETAILS OF WHAT YOU MEAN TO USE ARE ARRANGED TO PRODUCE *ONLY THE EFFECT YOU WANT!*

The reason for this warning is that certain divinatory patterns — *those of the I Ching, of Geomancy and of the Tarot especially* — are powerful to PRODUCE, not only within your psyche but also in the Astral World at large, THOSE CONDITIONS WHICH THEY REPRESENT.

You will thus be calling upon the Light of your Higher Self to activate and to confirm an extremely potent image.

The reason why these divinatory patterns can take effect in a "reverse manner," so to speak, and can not only *show* an existing condition but can also *produce* a condition where it did not exist, is really very simple when you call to mind the relationship of the Astral World to our emotions and instincts. A physical gesture or attitude can *represent* an emotion, but can also *produce* it.

Consider this. Two actors, representing characters which are unknown to you, appear on the stage. One character taunts the other. Will the second character accept this? The actor representing that second character squares his shoulders, stiffens his knees, inflates his chest. You know he will NOT accept the affront.

Now: do you ever accept a situation "lying down," which you afterwards regret and feel you ought to have contested it? If so, try the following next time! (If this sort of situation *never* happens to you, you will probably recognize the following as your natural reaction to a challenge.)

Push your knees back so that the joints are rigid, take a deep breath to inflate your chest fully, square your shoulders and press your elbows into your sides so as to flex your upper arm muscles. "Stiffen the sinews, summon up the blood," as Shakespeare's Henry V puts it. *Now how docile do you feel?*

Likewise in the world of symbol, that which can *represent* a condition can (if it be a true symbol) also *produce* the same condition. Usually a condition so produced will, certainly, be very transient: BUT NOT WHEN THE LIGHT OF THE HIGHER SELF ACTIVATES IT! Hence the need for caution.

Let us take an example of the effective use of a symbol from the I Ching, the "Book of Changes." Not only do the sixty-four "hexagrams" (six-lined diagrams) of the I Ching represent the continual fluctuations of the life-force as seen by the ancient Chinese wisdom of Tao, but also, as used in divination, the hexagram "drawn" will present an answer to a particular question asked by a particular person at a particular moment. The hexagram as a whole will present certain aspects of the matter in the light of the ancient Taoist wisdom of China (frequently aspects overlooked by the questioner although the symbolism of the hexagram usually reassures him as to its relevance) and, often, one or more of the lines of the hexagram will be indicated as carrying a specific "message."

Characteristically, it is these "message" lines which are denoted as being about to change, and thereby to produce the next hexagram relating to the subject; so a look at that further hexagram is also desirable in interpreting the situation.

Now, let us suppose that a girl is critically sick, and that a man who is familiar with the I Ching determines to use it in Creative Visualization on her behalf. Leafing through the Book of Changes he finds many lines which relate to a good outcome for this or that type of endeavour, but most of them, whether in their literal sense or in their traditional interpretation, would seem to apply to other kinds of situation.

He finally decides upon Hexagram 34, the TA KWANG hexagram, *The Power of the Great* or *The Symbol of Great Vigor.* Its image is that of thunder-energy moving harmoniously with the growth-energy of the heavens in springtime. The action is therefore auspicious.

Considering the individual lines of this hexagram, he finds one — the fourth — which carries a meaning well suited to his purpose. *"Right resolution produces good fortune. Cause for regret vanishes. The barrier yields, with no further opposition; the force applied has been like the leverage of a mighty wagon."*

Reading this, the man feels that the Light of his Higher Self will indeed produce, by its invisible might, the release of the girl from her sickness.

Before proceeding, however, he looks to see what will happen when this designated line changes, as change it must after being fulfilled:—

This is, in fact, the change from Hexagram 34 to Hexagram 11, the T'AI hexagram, *Harmony.* It shows the powers of heaven and earth acting together, the spiritual within the material, for natural growth and prosperity. Our friend will not be *visualizing* this further hexagram, but it is helpful to know that it represents the natural outcome of the action he will be undertaking. He can, with his experience of the I Ching and of its attunement to the life-forces, proceed in complete security.

The I Ching used in visualization for healing

For some time, therefore, he contemplates Hexagram 34, reflecting especially upon the fourth line, its spiritual power, and its action from within the hexagram so as to apply "hidden" leverage. Then he closes his eyes and visualizes this hexagram. He visualizes it as being over the girl's head. He encloses the whole design — the hexagram and the girl's head — within a circle of white. The hexagram has its "moving line" marked in the traditional way. The girl is happy and well. He fills himself with the Light of his Higher Self, then visualizes this light filling the whole picture in the circle (the girl and the hexagram) while fading from himself. Both the girl and the hexagram radiate light which fills the circle.

The man holds this picture in visualization for the space of several complete Rhythmic Breaths, then *"sends" it in the girl's direction,* remaining stationary until it has faded from sight.

Again, supposing a person selects a hexagram simply for his or her own benefit, then ONLY the hexagram — with its "changing line(s)" denoted — will be visualized, encircled, and charged, and this will subsequently be *contemplated, then allowed to fade from sight.*

With regard to the figures of Geomancy, there is little that need be said about the choice and Creative Visualization of one of them; it is done on similar lines to the above, according as it is for oneself or for someone else. Use of the Tarot in this way, however, is more complex.

Certainly there are circumstances in which anyone who is fully proficient in the understanding and interpretation of the Tarot (especially if this understanding is backed by a real grasp of the astrological principles involved) can feel sure that the influence denoted by one single card, whether of the Major or the Minor Arcana, is "just what is needed" to gain a desired result for the practitioner or for somebody else. In such circumstances, all that will be needed is to single out the card, to reflect upon its significance, then (on one's own behalf) to visualize it, or (on another person's behalf) to visualize it above the head of the person in question. The encircling, and the charging with the Light of the Higher Self, are then to proceed as we have given for the use of a hexagram of the I Ching.

Most often, however, it will be more satisfactory, more accurate and safer, to employ a spread of Tarot cards rather than any one card alone.

For use in connection with Creative Visualization, it is neither necessary nor desirable to have a very elaborate Tarot spread. The "ten-card spread" (well known by several names) allows sufficient scope for most situations to be represented in their past and present, inner and outer aspects, with, of course, the future — that is in this context the *willed* — outcome. This spread also has the advantage that cards from both Major and Minor Arcana, or the Major alone, can be employed.

The best approach to this is to consider the state of
things you wish to deal with by Creative Visualization,
and then to choose the cards and set them out in *the
Tarot spread you would most wish to see if you were
doing a reading on this situation.* Reflect upon it, upon
the interaction of its various parts. If you are experienced with the Tarot, you will not find a ten-card spread
difficult to memorize. Know it thoroughly.

Now proceed as we have described for the other
examples. DON'T TRY TO VISUALIZE EVERY DETAIL
OF THE CARDS IN YOUR SPREAD! You know what
they are, and there can be no doubt about them. (Everything you have ever seen or known is *there,* even if you
don't consciously recall it, and a good hypnotist could
accurately get at it. The perfect image, and implications,
of the Tarot spread you have just constructed and have
been reflecting upon is *there, right on the surface,* for use
in the way you intended.) If it is for yourself, "see" the
spread alone; if it is for another person, "see" the person
below the spread. Make your circle, and continue with
your Creative Visualization, as we have described.

We repeat — the use of divinatory methods to bring
about desired results is *only for those already familiar
with those methods.* If you want to use the I Ching, Tarot,
Geomancy, or any other method, you must learn it from
books and/or from a teacher AND from your own experience before you can use it effectively for Creative Visualization. *DO YOU WANT TO RE-WIRE AN ELECTRIC
CIRCUIT? THE SAME COMMON SENSE APPLIES!*

Checkpoint

6

- Plan a step at a time in your Creative Visualization career, besides having an overall objective.

- Practice the Charging Technique exactly as given in this chapter and go on practicing it.

- If you wish to use this technique on behalf of another person, visualize that person having the benefit you intend, then after charging and contemplating the image, "send" it by an act of will to the person concerned.

- For each work of Creative Visualization which is to employ the normal use of the Charging Technique, whether for yourself or for someone else, bring your project right through the "Foundation Work" from its beginning. *The "Foundation Work" is summarized on pages 122 and 123, paragraphs (a) through (f).*

• When you have begun using the Charging Technique on a particular Creative Visualization project, do this once daily and *persevere* until you attain your objective.

• If you have a favorite method of divination, explore its use in Creative Visualization as described in this chapter (pages 135 through 142). *You do not need to bring such operations through the preliminary stages of "Foundation Work" but you should be regularly practicing filling yourself with the Light of your Higher Self.*

• Take especial note of your first success with Creative Visualization. Think about it, derive confidence from it.

Study Points

7

Your Conscious Self is not alone! Your Higher Self will respond to your proper invocation. You need not be a "victim of chance" — the Universe is filled with free energy, and the Laws of the Universe can be directed to satisfy your needs and desires.

While this world we live in appears "dual" (up-down, light-dark, self-other), you can contact the Unity of Higher Forces and stop the "swing of the pendulum" so that what flows IN need not flow OUT.

The Star Technique is an excellent starter, getting you the initial opportunities that can be used as stairway steps in the Master Method.

The Multiplication Technique invokes the power of the Higher Self to increase things you already possess.

Star-Points and Multiplication

7

In the past chapter, you have been given the Master Method of Creative Visualization. That method involves also an "act of faith" in your Higher Self, and you may have known at once that this was just the STRAIGHT ROAD you were looking for.

Or you may ask, "Will that method work for me?"

OF COURSE IT WILL, and every moment spent in bringing it (or rather, in bringing *yourself*) to the point where THIS METHOD IS WORKING FOR YOU is *time well spent.*

All the same, you may (as when climbing a hill) feel you'd like to go roundabout a little before venturing that "straight road." You may feel you'd like to begin by playing for smaller stakes, just to prove to yourself that Creative Visualization is "for real."

THAT'S OKAY, IF IT'S THE WAY YOU FEEL.

AS SOON AS EVER YOU CAN PICTURE WHAT
YOU NEED, you can PROVE that there REALLY IS an
invisible force which will *bring it to you!*

In this chapter you will be given two simple alter-
natives to charging a visualized objective, which have
been TRIED AND PROVED by many, many people.
The first doesn't even name the Higher Self.

In Chapter One you read of a girl who longed to
live in a foreign land, and how she obtained this by the
"Star Technique" of Creative Visualization. Here is
another story, of a man named Stan who got JUST
WHAT HE VISUALIZED by this method, even though
at the time he began visualizing there seemed to be no
chance of it.

Stan was a skilled fitter of domestic radiators.
He was married and had three young children, so he was
not in a position to find fault with his job; nor, indeed,
would he have found any fault with it, except that to
him it was intolerably dull.

What he wanted was to be a humorous artist. From
boyhood he had filled notebook after notebook with
comic sketches of people and situations; he saw humor
all over the place, but now he kept those notebooks
well hidden away. Better, he felt sure, not to let anyone
think he took his job — or the foreman — less than
seriously!

Then he came across the Star Technique of Visualization. AND IT MIGHT HAVE BEEN MADE FOR HIM!

Visualizing himself doing drawing after drawing, and receiving praise and money for them, was not at all difficult for him. But, further, the system met his concern for his wife and children, his determination that they should not suffer for his ambitions, and on the other hand his certainty that his ambitions were *right*. Why, after all, did he have this talent and urge to draw if he wasn't to use it? HE *WOULD* BE A HUMOROUS ARTIST!

After less than a month of the Star Method, one day he was called into the office by one of the managers. He was told the firm wanted to produce a new handbook for trainee fitters. With his experience he would know all the pitfalls they should avoid. He could explain useful points to one of the advertising men who would do the text; then they'd illustrate it with humorous drawings —

"But I could do the drawings," said Stan, "and I know what all the different fittings and problems look like; instead of just *talking to* the man who will write the text, I can *explain my drawings to him!"*

"Let's see some drawings, then," said the manager.

So Stan drew a tank thoughtlessly installed in a remote corner of a loft, and the householder (with a wildly slopping bucket of water) putting a leg through the plaster as he went to top up the tank; then he drew a fur-coated, shivering lady standing amid stacks of unused lagging, gazing sadly at the burst and dripping pipes . . .

So he got the job of illustrating the new handbook (with a special bonus for doing it). And since the manager had a relative who was in education, not long afterwards there was a chance to do some Road Safety pictures. And then one thing led to another, without Stan having to give up his regular job at all; now he had an outside interest, he no longer found it tedious. His family, too, enjoyed the "little extras."

The chief difference, as you will notice, between the Star Technique and the Charging Technique is that *the Star Technique has no specific "charging" with the Light of the Higher Self.* There is a simple visualization of that which you desire, and then there is a sequence of simple actions together with the utterance (aloud or silently) of certain affirmations. The fulfillment of your desire will thus be ASTRALLY brought into being, while the Star's "points" (in both senses of the word) do in fact link your aspiration and your activity with the power and the attributes of the Higher Self.

Thus, although we do not make quite the claims and statements about this technique which we make about the complete Master Method, *yet we know that the Star Technique is VERY POWERFUL,* and that by its use you will gain plenty of evidence and insight on THE REALITY OF THE SPIRITUAL FORCE UNDERLYING CREATIVE VISUALIZATION. You will KNOW, after experiencing the benefits of Creative Visualization, that *YOUR CONSCIOUS SELF IS NOT ALONE IN THE STRUGGLES OF THIS WORLD.*

At the same time, by the Star Technique you may not always gain more than *a sample, an opportunity.* By this method, what you create astrally may not always be lasting in the material world; a lot depends on the supportive work you put into it. *(You should in any case be practicing the Foundation Work so as to be proficient in the full Master Method in due course!)* The girl we mentioned in Chapter 1 *learned to use the language of the country she wanted to go to.* This also was a sensible thing to do: ANYTHING YOU USE IS MORE LIKELY TO REMAIN YOURS. Stan had been able to draw funny pictures from when he was a boy, *and he had kept it up, however secretly.* What these people gained from the Star Method was an OPPORTUNITY.

This is important. The world is full of opportunities, and often we see these go to people who don't particularly want or need them. WHY? *We know why!*

NOTHING SUCCEEDS LIKE SUCCESS

UNTO EVERY MAN THAT HATH SHALL BE GIVEN

Life's like that. Most likely you yourself are offered opportunities you don't want, or which, if you were to accept them, might even twist your life into a totally unwelcome course. Yet those very chances might be a dream come true for another person — who, instead, is offered the one and only thing, maybe, that YOU need! (Not that such a disaster is necessarily final. Think of the boy who was offered the apartment Annie Z. wanted. Think of that other girl we have been discussing, who began with a vacation in a place she didn't care for.)

So what you need, first, no matter whether your material possessions are much or little, is to be put in the SUCCESS position for *the kind of opportunities YOU want and CAN USE.* That is one way in which the Star Method can be an excellent *"ice-breaker"* for you!

Other ways in which the Star Technique can help you include dealing with a health problem that may be holding you back, or solving a money problem, or helping you fulfill a promise you have made in good faith. The "Star" is well suited to getting you through such emergencies, and, above all, to securing your initial successes in Creative Visualization. *You should, however, work onward to the Charging Technique for consistent progress in life, no matter what good things you obtain by the Star Technique.*

A FATHER GIVES HIS CHILDREN CANDIES WHEN THEY ARE SMALL, TO SHOW THEM HE'S A REAL PAL. BUT WHEN THEY ARE BIGGER, HE HOPES FOR GENUINE FRIENDSHIP WITH THEM.

YOU SHOULD BE WILLING, AS TIME GOES ON, TO BUILD UP A REAL RELATIONSHIP WITH YOUR HIGHER SELF. THAT IS SOMETHING FAR GREATER THAN "GOODIES."

Now let us look at the diagram opposite, and see how to use the Star Technique.

(For your personal use EMPLOY YOUR OWN COPY OF THIS DIAGRAM; DON'T USE THE ONE IN THIS BOOK! Color your diagram; it should be YOURS ONLY.)

The Star Technique of Creative Visualization

Copyright © 1980 by Melita Denning & Osborne Phillips

The Star Technique of Creative Visualization

Use this procedure only ONCE DAILY, preferably first thing in the morning *or* last thing at night. (At other sessions, do your Foundation Work.)

Make all the preparations carefully.

Have the diagram ready to hand.

Sit with spine erect, legs parallel to each other.

Relax physically, and at the same time clear your mind of all intrusive thoughts or images.

Commence the Rhythmic Breath.

While sitting and breathing thus, reflect upon — and visualize as clearly as you can — *the objective for which you are carrying out this procedure, and the main reason(s) why you want it.* Be very clear about this, and *don't let your mind wander to other wants or wishes.* Everything in due order!

When you are ready, take up the diagram and look reflectively at the Heart in the top ray of the Star. It represents your heart, your desire! Say *nothing* at this moment, however, but TURN THE DIAGRAM A LITTLE so that the ray with the Scales is at the top. Looking at this, say slowly and deliberately:

BLESSED ARE THE LAWS OF THE UNIVERSE.

Say this sincerely, getting it through to all the levels of your psyche. "Laws" are not always popular; but it is JUST BECAUSE THESE LAWS EXIST THAT YOUR

CREATIVE VISUALIZATION WILL WORK; it is BY UTILIZING THE LAWS OF THE UNIVERSE that you will ensure you are NO MORE a "victim of CHANCE!" So you see these Laws to be *holy* and *the source of your happiness,* and you declare them BLESSED.

Now again TURN THE DIAGRAM SLIGHTLY, so that the ray of the Star showing the Horn of Plenty is at the top. Looking at this, say slowly and deliberately:

BLESSED IS ITS BOUNDLESS PLENTY.

This needs no elucidation! When you look at all the countless living beings in the world around you, and again at the colossal manifestations of free energy in electric storms, surging oceans, volcanoes; then, through the microscope, see worlds more of living creatures of which you would not otherwise be aware, or through the electronic microscope view the pulsating energic structure of matter itself; or when, again, the telescope reveals worlds, suns, galaxies which you experience only as a silvery dust in the night skies; ALL THIS IS PART OF THE UNIVERSE IN WHICH YOU LIVE, and can you doubt there is room in it for *your* life, *your* ambitions? So, truly, you should bless its boundless Plenty!

NOW TURN THE STAR AGAIN, so that the ray with the flying bird is at the top. The bird is flying towards you. You should *never* set a time-limit for the fulfillment of a Creative Visualization project (just as you should never specify a material source of supply) but YOU DO WANT TO SET THE WHEELS TURNING WITH REASONABLE SPEED! —so this is a point where you are not merely *accepting what is,* you are *affirming what is to be:*

BLESSED IS THE SWIFTNESS WITH WHICH ALL SHALL BE WROUGHT.

Now, you do not want anyone *harmed* by the fulfillment of your desire. Even if what you want is the restoration of something that another person cheated you of, BEWARE! DON'T WISH HARM TO THAT PERSON! This is NOT a matter of "morality." Morally, you might be quite justified, especially if lack of the thing has caused any kind of suffering to you, or to others through you. But, to put it in a figurative way, you don't want to invoke the natural "swing of the pendulum," BE-CAUSE A PENDULUM KEEPS ON SWINGING! You *don't* want to have to suffer further in your turn. If you don't want to believe the Buddha, the Christ or the Prophet of Islam, at any rate *believe the physicists*: you are living in *that kind of universe.* In this book we are only looking at it from a rather deeper point of view than that of the physicists, but THERE ARE NO CONTRADICTIONS.

What you need to do, therefore, is to bring in a higher force to *stop the swing of the pendulum,* at the point, of course, where you want it stopped. (Higher forces, fortunately, are intelligent forces!) So you TURN THE STAR so that the ray with the Shining Sun is at the top, and you say:

BLESSED IS THE TOTAL GOOD IN WHICH ALL
SHALL BE ACHIEVED.

"The Sun shines on the just and on the unjust alike." *WILL your gain to be nobody's loss!*

Now TURN THE STAR ONCE MORE, so that the ray with the Heart is again at the top, and complete your circle by saying:

BLESSED IS MY DESIRE FOR IT IS EVEN NOW
FULFILLED.

Say it boldly and with deep confidence. In the spiritual world it is EVEN NOW true, and —

Certainly
    Liberally
        Speedily
            Benignly
                Satisfyingly —

it shall be made manifest as true IN THE MATERIAL WORLD. All you have to do is continue placidly with the Star Method, *as nearly as possible at the same time every day* and (need we add?) *not discussing it with anyone.*

In Chapter 6 we pointed out that you should *never tell other people the details* of your Creative Visualization projects, and you should *avoid making people feel jealous or resentful* of your progress in life. The reason for these warnings is, to a great extent, the very evident one of *not inviting people's destructive emotions to combat your creative ones.* Even your nearest and dearest can, unfortunately, make problems in this way, if they (a) find it impossible to believe you have any inner faculties, or (b) unconsciously resent the fact that you *do have* an inner, and separate, life.

But there are two other, greater, reasons against talking about — and especially against *boasting about* — anything you hope to achieve by Creative Visualization. One is a matter of STRESS.

Stress in the right place is a very good thing. If you want to shoot an arrow from a bow, the bowstring has to be pulled tight. *No stress, no flight.* If you want a spring-operated clock to tell the time, you have to wind it up so that the spring exerts pressure on the wheels. *No stress, no action.*

Now: the Material World is the most difficult of worlds in which to produce effective action, and the reason for this difficulty is, quite simply, THE INERTIA OF MATTER. You can quite easily create an image of what you want in the Astral World. To cause a lasting change in the Material World, however, you must ENERGIZE YOUR ASTRAL WORLD SPIRITUALLY,

TO CREATE A STRESS which will COMPEL action in the Material World. By *talking about* the desired result, therefore, you are in danger of RELEASING THE TENSION in a way which is of no use to you. (Quite often, of course, it is this tension itself which makes you feel "impelled" to talk about the project; so here is particular need for care!)

There is another danger. The standards by which most of us judge ourselves, especially for anything which smacks of vanity, folly, weakness, are far more severe than the judgments of any external God! We can't easily alter these judgments, however irrational we consider them to be, because they are usually embedded deep in the submerged unconscious strata which relate to our "formative years." We can, therefore, be making an obstacle for ourselves, when we come directly or by implication to ask our Higher Self to ratify, to give full reality to, our image-making, IF WE HAVE MADE OURSELVES FEEL NEEDLESSLY GUILTY ABOUT THIS MATTER BY BOASTING OF IT.

TO KEEP SILENCE IS TO MAINTAIN THE INTEGRITY, NOT ONLY OF THE OPERATION BUT ALSO OF OUR SELF-RESPECT.

However, you can always tell your friends and dear ones, if they are troubled about a situation you are working on, that they should be hopeful, optimistic, should build up their own creative thoughts and images. In that way, you will be helping them; and also, without saying so, HELPING THEM TO HELP YOU.

We shall pass on now to consideration of another technique which is also not so great as the complete Master Method of Creative Visualization but which is, in the proper circumstances for its use, OF HIGH POTENCY.

This particular technique is *directly dependent on your ability to fill yourself with the Light of your Higher Self,* but it does not require a fully developed ability to visualize. In a different way from the Star Technique, therefore, it can be of great use to you before you are competent in all the Foundation Work. It is especially designed for the kind of situation where *you have some of what you want but not enough.* IT CAN THUS BE VERY HELPFUL INDEED.

You may have a place to live, but need a larger place. You may have some money, but not enough for your project. You may have clothes, but need new clothes. SOMETHING YOU HAVE MAY NOT BE ADEQUATE FOR ITS PURPOSE, OR YOU FEAR THE SUPPLY MAY COME TO AN END.

In such a situation, it is important to know quite clearly WHAT TO DO. There are people who have picked up a fragment of the truth without understanding it, who are in the habit of telling us we should *be content with what we have.* (Generally, the less a person has, the more often that person is told to be content with it.)

Now, this statement that we should be content with what we have *is not false.* But it is that dangerous and misleading thing, A SMALL PART OF THE TRUTH.

The real truth is this:
Don't hate what you have!
Don't despise what you have!
Don't fear that what you have will let you down!
What you have is A WAY TO SOMETHING BETTER!

But to achieve this, you must not smash what is there already; you must cherish it, cleanse or purify it if need be, but sustain it, LOVE IT. In this matter of Creative Visualization, remember, we are not only dealing with this material world; we are also dealing with those levels where the happenings of this world are shaped and formed. And the values of those levels are important in this material world. HATE AND FEAR DESTROY. LOVE AND TRUST CREATE. You will see this.

Many men and women have achieved great good from what they saw as a totally unsatisfactory state of affairs. They were in that sense DISCONTENTED. But they did not waste time and energy lamenting over the shortcomings of THE MEANS AND OPPORTUNITIES WHICH CAME TO HAND. They used these things (*What else could they use?*) TO ACHIEVE WHAT THEY DESIRED.

Behind the lives and achievements of such people is *a spiritual force far greater, far higher, than any of its manifestations in the material world*. The finest earthly achievements are only a dark shadow of the spiritual force which underlies them, because *WHEN YOU WORK WITH YOUR HIGHER SELF, THE POWER, SPLENDOR, AND NOBILITY OF THE FORCE ON WHICH YOU DRAW ARE TRULY ILLIMITABLE.*

The Bible, both in the Old Testament and in the New, gives stories which illustrate the working of this force, but *only so far as its visible effects in this world are concerned.* The PRINCIPLE is not given. None the less, people have loved these stories through the centuries, because many have *known and proved* that such things happen. Read the story of the Prophet Elijah and the widow, and her small supply of food, in the First Book of Kings, Chapter 17 verses 9 through 16. Read also, in the New Testament, the story of the feeding of the multitude with loaves and fishes. Several tellings of it are given: Matthew chapter 15 verses 35 through 38; Mark chapter 6 verses 35 through 44 *and* chapter 8 verses 1 through 10; Luke chapter 9 verses 12 through 17.

It is from these stories that the ensuing technique is called *The Multiplication Technique.* (There is also the consideration of the arithmetical type of multiplication. Multiply any number by something, and you get something. Multiply any number by zero, and you get zero. You must start with *something* to use this method, your pinch of meal and drop of oil, but SOMETHING. Otherwise, you need the other methods.)

But, for the pure dazzling spiritual insight and inspiration of the divine truth underlying these happenings, read — and ponder upon — the following words from an eighteenth-century Persian mystical poet, Ahmed Hatif. He is not, of course, referring to earthly matters. Take the words first in their full spiritual impact:—

WHEN ALL THINGS THAT YOU SEE,
SEE YOU WITH LOVE,
THEN ALL THINGS THAT YOU LOVE,
SOON WILL YOU SEE.

Dwell upon this. It is not "too high" for you, because it is a great spiritual truth and therefore, when you let its meaning seep through your mind and soul without resistance, you will find it COMES NATURAL-LY TO YOU.

And what is true on the highest levels must also be true upon earth, because THERE IS ONLY ONE SPIRITUAL TRUTH.

Don't make any mistakes about "love." Love is not possessiveness, or weakness, or emotionalism. It involves seeing-the-best-in, helping-develop-naturally. This often applies to things, to events, as well as to living beings you may be responsible for.

It also applies to YOURSELF. It means practicing seeing yourself as essentially YOU, finding out what you sincerely want and building, visualizing, for *that* (and for things which fit into that) instead of maybe changing your line every time the media come up with a new attraction.

Also — and this is important — WITH THAT KNOWL-EDGE, YOU WILL NOT TREAD ON OTHER PEOPLE'S TOES AS YOU DO WHEN BLUNDERING AROUND. YOU CAN CONFIDENTLY "LIVE AND LET LIVE." *YOU KNOW THERE IS PLENTY IN THE UNIVERSE FOR ALL.* YOU CAN LIVE ACCORDINGLY!

The Multiplication Technique

Stand. (You may possibly need to walk about soon, blessing various objects in a room for instance.)

Establish your Rhythmic Breathing.

Look at what you want increased, or at some of it.

If you cannot clearly visualize, at least *suppose* a white circle around what you are looking at; a boundary simply to what is to be included in the intended operation.

Think clearly of what you are looking at as being WHAT YOU NEED; whether as "larger," "newer," "adequate," or as precisely "$. . ."

Fill yourself with the Light of your Higher Self, as described in Chapter 4.

Charge *the actual object* with this Light: that is, in your mind imagine and affirm its radiance growing in and transfusing the object, making it luminous, while at the same time gradually fading from yourself. When the transfer is complete, say:

GOOD AND SUFFICIENT TO ME IS MY (whatever).

IN THE POWER OF MY HIGHER SELF I BLESS IT.

IN JOY AND PLENTY I POSSESS IT!

Contemplate the radiant object awhile, then let the Light slowly fade from your awareness.

Keeping up your Rhythmic Breathing, repeat this procedure of looking, charging and blessing upon any other objects that are to be included.

Perform this daily. It is powerful for increase!

Checkpoint

7

- If you don't feel ready for the complete Master Method, you can nevertheless benefit by minor techniques.

- If you have difficulty in Charging with the Light of the Higher Self, you can still use the Star Technique of Creative Visualization.

- For the Star Technique, copy the diagram from this chapter to make your own personal diagram. This will be individually yours, for YOUR Creative Visualization. (You can color it too if you wish.)

- If you have difficulty in visualizing, you can still benefit from the Power of your Higher Self through the Multiplication Technique.

- Since you should in any case be practicing the Foundation Work daily, you ought to build this up for your objective so as to prepare for and strengthen your use of Star Technique or Multiplication Technique.

Study Points

8

You are a "whole" person of Mind, Body and Spirit.

The Creative Plan of Relaxation provides the basis for a program of Inner Development.

The same techniques of Creative Visualization can be applied to memory-training and habit-change.

Dare to Be Powerful!

8

On going through the book, several ideas may have occurred to you which should be considered at this point.

You may, for instance, want something for yourself which cannot easily be visualized, such as the power to stop smoking, to give up alcohol or excessive eating or some other thing, or to be an early riser.

This chapter will help with these and similar matters.

Or you may only have wanted to obtain a number of material things by Creative Visualization, and our repeated references to your Higher Self may have been surprising or even slightly embarrassing.

The fact is, whether you want something spiritual or mental or something material, YOU are not just a spirit or just a body; YOU are a living, complete PERSON.

To function well in the material world, you need to enlist the help of your mind and spirit.

To function well at mental and spiritual levels, you need the co-operation of your physical body.

We have shown how you can, up to a point, do Creative Visualization quite effectively without direct reference to any High Power, by whatever name. We do however bring in the Higher Self, because:

(a) Your Higher Self is, FOR YOU, the source of all abundance, and you should know It as a friend.

(b) Goods and benefits obtained through Creative Visualization should be SAFEGUARDED to be as enduring as they ought in the material world.

The necessary SAFEGUARDS for the durability of these goods and benefits are, *first,* that they should be infused with the Power of the Higher Self, and *second,* that they should be put to good use without delay.

That brings us to another point for consideration. A person may make considerable progress in Creative Visualization. The potential supply of benefits which can be obtained by this means is, in itself, LIMITLESS; but how much does that person have the capacity TO USE BENEFICIALLY?

THIS IS A VITAL QUESTION. *THE CAPACITY FOR USE IS, ULTIMATELY, THE MEASURE OF WHAT CAN BE OBTAINED.*

Therefore, even to be able to advance progressively in the material world, it is good that you should be able to open up and develop your inner resources. And conversely, if your first desire is for a greater development of inner resources, this in turn will bring the need for greater outward means of expression, of adventure and experiment, *to use your abilities.*

All the foregoing reflections lead to one same conclusion. No matter whether your initial wants be outward or inward, some degree of alternation between the two types of development is needed for satisfactory progress. *Build in steps!* (See page 116).

In this book, so far, you have been given:

THE MASTER METHOD OF CREATIVE VISUALIZA-
TION: Foundation Work and Charging Technique.

THE STAR TECHNIQUE, which may be used as an alternative to the Charging Technique.

THE MULTIPLICATION TECHNIQUE, which needs no visualization of the objective but requires that you already possess this objective to some extent.

You have also been given (in Chapter 2) THE CREA-
TIVE PLAN OF RELAXATION.

The Creative Plan of Relaxation provides the basis for your program of inner development, whether this development is concerned with entirely mental and spiritual qualities or with the interaction of mind and body. Already, as you have it, this Plan of Relaxation involves not only physical control, but a directed well-wishing of each bodily part. *That is what makes it CREATIVE.*

Only YOU can formulate your program for inner development. We can give positive advice on so doing, but you know your needs and you know yourself from the inside AS NOBODY ELSE CAN.

For this, practice Creative Relaxation DAILY.

For example: say you want to stop smoking. Now, as a matter of fact the very best way to do this is to announce firmly to yourself that smoking is DONE WITH — OUT — NEVER AGAIN! — with no reasons given and no room for doubt or hesitation. (This is good for many other things besides smoking.) If you can crown a session of Creative Relaxation by making that announcement when you are fully in harmony and at peace with yourself, you need never look back. You should, indeed, never even consider looking back.

If however you have made this resolution in the past, then doubted, hesitated, felt regretful *and given up,* you have this time to proceed more gradually.

There are three rules to observe.

1.   Keep mentally and physically busy (NOT overworked) with something which really interests you. Your program of Foundation Work should fulfill this need. This should keep your attention effectively *off* any "withdrawal symptoms" whether physical or psychological, until the symptoms fade out. (You can get medication to clear your system of nicotine. But this will only help you stop smoking if you at the same time take care of the very real emotional aspect.)

2.   Sort out your chief incentive for smoking (it may be imitativeness, a conversational opening or defense, part of a sex routine, a way of ending a meal, or something you just do from fear of seeming unsociable or from fear of criticism. Unfortunately, the lung-cancer ads have made a lot of people scared to stop for fear of seeming timorous. Or, of course, you may have made a habit of smoking to aid decision-making, and gone on even though you have found it doesn't).

Above all, pin down any inclination to be sentimental about it, whether in self-pity, dislike of saying "no" to a friend or partner, or identification of smoking as part of your life-style.

3.   Sort out your chief incentive for NOT smoking. At the present stage, you are working this out rationally for your own benefit; you are not putting the case to your instinctual and emotional nature, so you should consider this matter *thoroughly.*

For practical use, however, you will realize that this rational argument, if you present it just as it stands, will probably be *thrown out* by your instinctual and emotional nature! You must work out how to give it IN SMALL DOSES, and with as much emotional "flavoring" as possible, until it is accepted.

You may be concerned for your health, or your money. You may be concerned because smoking is no part of a natural life-style. You may love a non-smoker.

4.   In your next daily session of Creative Relaxation, work as usual right through the final stage, with *great care* over the blessing of each part of your body.

I CARE FOR MY BODY.
I TRULY LOVE MYSELF.
GOODWILL, STRENGTH AND BLESSING TO
EVERY PART!

Continue to lie relaxed in that blissful state of inner unity in which this practice culminates, but after a pause *instill another idea*. According to your motivation, it might be for example,

MY BODY DOES MUCH FOR ME
MY NERVOUS SYSTEM DOES MUCH FOR ME
I DO NOT WISH TO POISON THEM IN RETURN

or maybe something like this:—

MONEY IS POWER TO LIVE
WHAT SHOULD IT BUY? POWER TO LIVE.

But it has to be something which is important to *you personally*. You should *keep it simple*, as it is meant to be absorbed by your Lower Unconscious levels.

5.   After a few sessions, *you should be able to add something more specific about smoking.*

If this is accepted by your emotional nature without any bad reaction, fine! Stay at this point for a couple of weeks to MAKE SURE of the absence of bad reaction, then you can go on to the next stage.

5A. What do we mean by a bad reaction? It would usually be an intensification, a stepping-up, of the emotional pressure upon you to do whatever it is you are trying to stop — in this case, smoking — without any clear rational reason as to why this should happen. That would mean the emotional nature fears it is about to be DEPRIVED of something.

Your rational mind may be quite aware that smoking bestows no benefit upon you in any way, but that doesn't ensure the emotional nature is aware of the same thing. You are dealing here with your SUB-RATIONAL self. It has its own "reasons," but these are emotional promptings, not rational reasons. Your emotional nature may believe smoking is adult, or looks prosperous, or steadies the nerves. (You may have seen the shaking hands of a heavy smoker, but your sub-rational self *is* sub-rational!) If there is a protest, GO BACK to the first stage, and add some words and ideas to put right whatever is the cause of the trouble. *As with a child, be patient, but firm.*

If any particular dream or waking impression comes to you when you are carrying out this kind of practice for whatever purpose, WRITE IT DOWN. It means something to *the sender*, if not to your rational mind.

By paying attention to these things you may find out that tied up among whatever emotion-reasons for smoking you were aware of, there has been one or more that would never even have crossed your mind. We all of us know we have a sub-rational self but it can still give us some surprises!

The next step, after anything of this sort has been de-fused by taking it out and looking at it in your present perspective (not unkindly, but as at an outgrown toy), is to tackle *the kind of situation* which, in your experience, prompts smoking.

6.   You have, *still in the last part of your daily session of Creative Visualization*, to build up a visualization of that situation. "LIVE" IT AS REALISTICALLY AS POSSIBLE, re-creating it in your imagination, be it a board meeting, a drink with the boys or a session of lovemaking — ONLY, IN THIS IMAGINATIVE LIVING THROUGH IT, YOU DON'T SMOKE. YOU VISUAL- IZE IT AS BEING A TOTAL SUCCESS WITHOUT SMOKING. You see yourself as the guy who only does what HE pleases and is respected for it, or as the gal whose elegance stands without any outmoded gimmick. (Or whatever is the key to the situation.)

THEN FILL YOURSELF WITH THE LIGHT OF YOUR HIGHER SELF. CHARGE AND BLESS THE VISUALIZED IMAGE OF YOURSELF, CONTEM- PLATE IT AWHILE, THEN LET IT FADE FROM SIGHT.

Take great care, *always,* with the details of the charging. You will have maintained your Rhythmic Breathing throughout the whole procedure of Creative Relaxation and your new formulation and visualization in the final section. Through several Rhythmic Breaths you proceed to fill yourself with the Light of your Higher Self, keeping up meanwhile your visualization of your *new, happy, successful non-smoking self* as described on the page facing this.

Now, in your visualization, you ring with a white line that happy image. And on a similar number of Rhythmic Breaths you see the image filling with the Light of your Higher Self so that the image radiates with intense white light which fills the circle, leaving your inner awareness.

Hold this radiant image in visualization, contemplating it through several Rhythmic Breaths; then slowly let it fade from your awareness. But remember — YOU HAVE CHARGED IT WITH THE LIGHT AND POWER OF YOUR HIGHER SELF, so it is still there, POWERFUL TO ACT UPON YOUR EMOTIONAL NATURE AND THOSE UNCONSCIOUS IMPULSES.

Here, in fact, we are given an opportunity to examine something of the deeper significance which makes the Charging Technique HIGHLY POTENT in such a matter as stopping smoking.

Remember: the Light of your Higher Self is POWER AND LIFE-FORCE AND LOVE AND BLESSING ALL IN ONE.

POWER ATTRACTS POWER. LOVE ATTRACTS LOVE.

So YOU — the NEW YOU — will not only be *more respected*, but MORE LOVED. YOU will not only be *more admired*, you will be MORE ATTRACTIVE.

How do you know this? How do you know you are not in fact loved "for your faults," for your weaknesses? Because the REAL YOU is, *as a fact*, far more lovable, attractive, able to be respected, than any of the more faulty images of you. Your nearest and dearest may not know this — but then, they haven't yet met the future, truer versions of you! WHEN THEY DO, THEY WILL MAKE NO MISTAKE.

So — *DARE* TO BE POWERFUL, LOVABLE, DYNAMIC! *LOVE YOURSELF, FORGIVE YOUR-SELF, LET YOURSELF GO FREE!*

When you build up that victorious image of the NEW YOU, before you charge it with the Light of your Higher Self,

PAUSE.

ENJOY CONTEMPLATING IT.

THAT IS YOURSELF!

You are going to live your life YOUR WAY, charged with Power and Life-force and Love and Blessing all in one. NOW CHARGE IT WITH THE LIGHT AND MAKE IT REAL.

We have given the plan of action for stopping smoking in some detail, partly because this in itself will be valuable to many people, and partly also because the method of proceeding is easily adaptable to individual needs for a number of other subject-areas.

Before leaving this topic, we will answer a question which is likely to be asked by a number of people who have one particular motivation for stopping smoking (or drinking or laziness or aggressiveness or whatever.)

The question is, *I have fallen in love with someone who doesn't do* (whatever), *who intensely dislikes* (whatever). *Because of my love for this person, I wish finally to stop* (whatever). *Do I have to go through the perhaps lengthy procedure you describe? Can't I take a short cut? Can't my love for this person inspire me to give up utterly what he/she dislikes?*

In the first place, as we have said, the procedure outlined in this chapter MAY NOT be a lengthy one. For some people, *one* session of Creative Visualization directed to the purpose may produce a total turnabout.

In other cases, however, there is more to be said.

How have you managed to fall in love with someone whose tastes apparently differ in this way from your own? And why do you want to follow that person's example in this particular way?

One possible way this situation can come about is through the question of smoking/not-smoking (as our example) having been only an incidental difference from your point of view, while the other person sees it as a vital issue and makes a condition of your conformity. This, frankly, stands about a 50% chance of success, because you either *do* or *don't* really want it, and neither Creative Visualization nor any other method has much chance of achieving for you something you don't really want.

A much better and more hopeful situation exists when you have had impulses, however slight, towards a viewpoint like that person's even before you met. That viewpoint may be one of the things you especially love and feel drawn to in him/her. It may be a viewpoint you would have adopted yourself if you could have been more strong-minded about it, and now you welcome this person's example and strength and you want to try again.

If that is the position, you should certainly *recognize this*, and follow it through as being YOUR desire, NOT as something you are doing to please your loved one or (worst of all) as an "offering" to secure his/her approval.

There are several good reasons for this. The main one is that altogether fundamental to the methods of Creative Visualization, as to other forms of inner development, is the knowledge that *what you do is to bring yourself nearer THE REAL YOU*, not someone else's idea of what you ought to be!

Creative Practice for a Better Memory

Can Creative Visualization or Creative Relaxation help improve your memory?

Certainly, if you realize (as for slimming or for bigger muscles, which you can also work for effectively) there is OUTER as well as INNER work to be done.

When you ask for a "better memory," do you mean the ability to remember certain set things, like your intended after-dinner speech or the terms of the Treaty of Vienna (1815) or the whole of *Friends, Romans, Countrymen?* Or the proper name for that thing on the dashboard you always call the gizmo? Or the date of your mother-in-law's birthday?

Or do you just want to be less absent-minded about things in general?

Before we come to the Creative part of memory improvement, let's look at the helpful exploration you should put in on it at other times. *Memory needs practice, but we are not going to ask you to exercise it on a lot of unnecessary material.*

You have heard of people whose digestive system gets into trouble because of insufficient "fiber." They may be taking in all the protein, vitamins, minerals they need, but there still has to be enough "fiber" for the digestive system *to take hold of.* MEMORY IS LIKE THAT TOO.

Teachers and instructors of all sorts sometimes make a big mistake about material to be memorized. They try to CUT IT DOWN, STREAMLINE it to such an extent that the student's memory has nothing *to take hold of.* So it can't function properly. While anything which GRIPS THE ATTENTION may ensure the text associated with it being remembered for evermore.

This "anything" may be quite trivial or unrelated to the subject-matter. But it will be better if your attention is gripped by something VITALLY CONNECTED WITH THE SUBJECT-MATTER YOU WANT TO REMEMBER; then your understanding as well as your memory will be aided, and each will help the other.

You will have something to fall back on if your memory lets you down.

Being aware of this will at once make your memory LESS LIKELY TO LET YOU DOWN.

Your After-Dinner Speech. There is probably no reason why you should memorize the exact words! You most likely only want to memorize the exact words because you fear that otherwise you may "dry up."

That's just the way to "dry up!"

Write down on a piece of paper the list of topics you want to talk about and the order in which you want to put them. There has to be a REASON for those topics and for that order. *Make sure you will not forget those reasons.*

Now learn your topics. BUT DON'T LEARN

YOUR SPEECH! NEVER LEARN THE EXACT WORDS UNLESS THE EXACT WORDS MATTER.

The reason? Well, if you can do without the exact words, *that's one thing less which might throw you.* If you depend on the words, and a phrase or a sentence escapes you, you are lost, "dried up;" but if you are following the sense of the topics, you can easily go on with *what you want to talk about.*

Another reason is this. You might compose a set speech of a certain length; you might plan it to be humorous or solemn. Then less or more time can be allowed you, from one cause or another, or a piece of unforeseen news turns a cheerful occasion to a solemn one or vice versa. How can you make an adaptation if each word is tied to the next?

At your daily session of Creative Relaxation, when the relaxation is completed and you are lying, breathing rhythmically, in inner and outer peace and harmony, *visualize the occasion on which you will make your speech.* Exact phrases may come into your mind; welcome them but don't try to imprison them. The important thing is to build up your sense of well-being, of ease, of SUCCESS. Go through the topics in your mind, in their right order; if you fail to recall one of them, *don't worry,* just go over your list in time to make sure you get it right tomorrow. (Or if a particular order refuses to be remembered, *is its logic wrong? Should you alter it?)*

Finally CHARGE YOUR VISUALIZED PICTURE OF SUCCESS: MAKE IT A LIVING REALITY.

The Treaty of Vienna (or any other massive piece of factual documentation you may have to learn for class or examination purposes).

Why is it considered desirable that you should learn these things? Not, usually, to find out if you have a solidly mechanical power of memorizing, although that too can have its value to anyone who means to stand the pace in, for instance, a university course.

The most satisfactory and reliable way of playing this game (whether it is a matter of the Treaty of Vienna or a matter of memorizing the melting-points of different alloys of aluminum, copper and manganese), is the way it is meant to be played. GET THE PICTURE INTO YOUR IMAGINATION. See where places like "Swedish Pomerania" were on the map, what use these places were to the powers that got them. Or see exactly what the different parts of your diagram mean with regard to the melting-points of the alloys. Whatever the subject may be, copy the map or the curve or whatever it is out of the book, or compile a diagram of your own, AND LIVE IN IT IN YOUR IMAGINATION. You can, if the subject is of the least interest to you.

And call to mind, too, that YOUR mind and brain and imagination are designed on much the same plan as the minds and brains and imaginations of other human beings who have found these things fascinating.

So, *first*, get to know your subject, not as words or as *figures*, but as *facts*. Then RELAX. VISUALIZE. CHARGE (it's part of your life!) and LEARN.

Friends, Romans, Countrymen. Sometimes, of course, exact words must be memorized and no substitute will be acceptable. But here too, you can make it much easier for yourself if you break the piece, or the play, down into sequences of thought: reasoning and emotion, interaction of characters, the whole background which gives rise to the words. This underlying *development* is, in the first place, easier to remember because your mind and your emotional nature will assimilate it more easily than your brain will be able to memorize a mechanical rote of words; then, when the development, the "story" in fact, is clear to you, the words will have a definite pattern of associations that your brain can relate them to.

So reach a point where you can, in the state of complete Creative Relaxation, "live" the whole sequence of events and/or the emotional and reasoned development of the piece; charge it with the Light of your Higher Self because (although you are neither Shakespeare nor Mark Antony) YOU are the actor whose success this is to be; *and then, afterwards, set about memorizing the words.* They will then, truly, "come to life" for you.

Many actors, actresses and dancers of a religious temperament have been seen before a performance invoking a blessing upon themselves in their own special way; then they have gone on stage and given a truly INSPIRED performance. *The spirit of the people in the audience naturally recognizes and responds to the spirit of the artist.*

General Forgetfulness ("absent-mindedness"). If the trouble is not due to concussion, stress-amnesia or another medically treatable disorder, it probably has that simplest of all causes of memory troubles in the young, the old, the learned, the unlearned, in fact all who have to any extent learned to think. Whether you have detected it or not, the root of these troubles is the habit of *thinking of one thing while doing something else.*

Therefore the thing thought about is not thought about properly; and the thing done is not done properly.

Because this *is* a habit, the only real cure for it is, very attentively, to set about establishing a contrary habit. When you think, GIVE FULL ATTENTION TO WHAT YOU ARE THINKING. If you write down notes about your thoughts, you probably will not be able to give attention to anything else meanwhile. When you carry out some physical activity, GIVE FULL ATTEN-TION TO WHAT YOU ARE DOING. If you walk, get full exercise value from walking. If you wrap a parcel, take an interest and a pride in doing it efficiently. When you speak to another person, *make sure that person gives full attention too.*

ALSO DO YOUR FOUNDATION WORK, AND CREATIVE RELAXATION, DAILY.

And in the last part of each session, while you lie fully relaxed, VISUALIZE THE MAIN INCIDENTS OF THE COMING DAY. SEE YOURSELF AS POSITIVE, ATTENTIVE, WITH-IT. *Circle, charge, contemplate the image, let it fade.*

The Gizmo. This is not usually a matter you need bring your Higher Self into, but the principle is otherwise much the same as for the preceding things.

With any machine that you have to do with, it's desirable that you should know what every visible bit is for, and what it connects up with under the dashboard, keyboard or outer casing. You don't have to take everything apart and look, but if you can find out just that much, most of the names you can be expected to know will either be self-evident or will be quite easy to memorize.

In the event that you have at any time to ask for a repair to your car, airplane, calculator or typewriter, there is a distinct advantage in being able to use the right words, to speak the right language for the purpose. It tells the technician at once that you are an intelligent person who understands something about your machine, and so you are not at all likely to have mishandled it. That way, you automatically lay claim to the best service. (That is simply a FACT.)

Family Birthdays. Here is an area in which you can well make full use of Creative Visualization techniques, in a way which will help and cheer all concerned; and the extent to which you go into it can depend entirely upon how much time you have to spare for it.

Many people try to deal with family birthdays and other anniversaries by writing them in a special diary or notebook. *Then they forget to look in the diary.*

The real trouble with these important dates, of course, is that they don't seem to connect up in any real way with the people concerned. Some people are better at remembering such dates than others, because they have a knack of finding and firmly attaching little facts which belong to their own personal world: "I never forget Aunt Suzie's birthday because it's always *just* too chilly for me to wear a summer dress," for example; or, "Jack's end-of-year presents, one for Christmas and one for his birthday, why, I'd never *dare* forget!"

BUT THERE IS A MUCH BETTER, POSITIVE AND CREATIVE WAY TO FIX THESE IMPORTANT DATES IN YOUR MIND — BECAUSE THEY *DO* HAVE A REAL LINK WITH THE PEOPLE CONCERNED!

Have you ever thought of looking into the astrological approach to the question? If you have even the slightest knowledge of astrology already, chances are that you don't need these paragraphs; every birthday is so good a pretext for a little research, that you most likely never forget one! But, to everyone to whom this is a novel idea, we must point out that we are not asking you to go very deeply into a fascinating but really limitless subject.

Start at the "shallow end," with a reliable text on sun-signs which will give you an insight into the importance of the various planets as well. Llewellyn's *Astrological Calendar* (published annually) is an excellent

Find a way to connect the birthday with the person!

and attractive starting point, while it also contains features which are valuable and even necessary to the more advanced.

With sun-sign character sketches only, however, you will inevitably find that while some of them fit some people you know as if they were personal portraits, some seem to be about half-right and others are only a faint likeness. The reason for this is that nobody is "entirely made up of his sun-sign," and the other factors in a horoscope can vary in prominence according to various controlling forces.

The chief cause which leads people to take up Astrology as a hobby, is that they are led by curiosity and by human interest to seek, and they do indeed find, confirmation of one of its components after another. No matter how long or how short the road you are prepared to travel with this, one of the finest books to carry you on the vital next stages from being able only to recognize a person's sun-sign to getting an intelligible astrological view of that person, is Grant Lewi's time-tested *Heaven Knows What.* When you have learned from this book the simplest astrological framework, it is packed with information for you.

Llewellyn's annual *Moon Sign Book* will also have many good things for you.

The point for us here is again to give your memory some "fiber" to take hold of. *When you really IDENTIFY someone with his/her birthday, you REMEMBER IT!*

You can, if you have a flair for it, put your findings into verse. (These are best kept to yourself as a rule, however kindly you mean them!) They don't have to be brilliant, but rhyme is an age-old and effective aid to memory; so you might produce this kind of thing —

April seventh, Auntie Mary's
Birthday puts her Sun in Aries:
Speaks her mind to man or mike.
(Better ask her what she'd like!)

Pa Brown's inventions are many and various:
He was born August One with the Moon in Aquarius.

Mom-in-law's birthday is November eight!
She's a charmer, she knows, but with sick folk she's great.

But now we come to the CREATIVE PART OF WHAT YOU CAN DO WITH THIS KNOWLEDGE. With a little of this knowledge, you can give someone A MUCH BETTER "BIRTHDAY WISH" THAN JUST A PRETTY CARD. (They'll appreciate a card too, naturally!)

You will remember the description in Chapter 6 of ways in which procedures usually employed for a divination can be employed also to PRODUCE A DESIRED EFFECT FOR A PERSON, by using that method in connection with Creative Visualization? (READ ON BEFORE YOU TURN BACK TO IT!)

Just as with the procedures mentioned in that chapter, you should not try to do anything advanced with the symbols of Astrology until you thoroughly understand what you are doing: but there is a difference.

The symbols of Astrology are not powerful in themselves as are, say, the I Ching symbols. The symbols of Astrology have the power you and other people of your culture give to them. Therefore, *provided you keep it simple,* if you have a strong power of visualization you can convey a potent blessing to someone by means of the symbols of Astrology, even before you know very much of Astrology. (YOU SHOULD BUILD THIS UP THROUGH THE "FOUNDATION WORK!")

Most people feel their sun-sign is "lucky" for them; it has, after all, effectively seen them into this life, and a person is "native" to his sun-sign as a fish is to the water or a bird to the air — or as Brer Rabbit to his briar-patch. It is a happy thought therefore to visualize and to charge with blessing on someone's birthday the appropriate zodiacal sign, or the emblem of the sign's ruling planet (with maybe its keyword such as *Prosperity* for Jupiter, *Stability* for Saturn and so on).

That is about as far as the beginner in Astrology should take it, visualizing the zodiacal or planetary sign above the head of the person in question, circling the whole image in white, charging it with the Light of the Higher Self and "sending" it to the recipient as a blessing. But more advanced study could open further paths. What about weddings, anniversaries, for instance?

Checkpoint

8

- The Creative Plan of Relaxation should be used daily for the "inner development" part of your Creative Visualization program.

- *To break an unwanted habit such as smoking:*
  1. Keep mentally and physically busy: Foundation Work helps here.
  2. Sort out your chief motivations for keeping this habit.
  3. Sort out your chief motivations against it.
  4. Introduce a simple, emotive GENERAL statement which harmonizes with your main objection to the habit, into the final stage of your daily Creative Relaxation.
  5. After a few sessions, introduce a simple emotive SPECIFIC statement against the habit.

5A. If your Lower Self opposes this by stepping up the habit, you must find out why your emotional nature clings to it. This involves examining your dreams.

6. When there is no opposing reaction, build up (still in the final stage of your daily Creative Relaxation) the typical situation in which you are most liable to this habit. "Live through" this in visualization but WITHOUT falling into the habit. Charge the visualized image of your victorious self.

• To improve your memory:
AVOID thinking about one thing while you do another. FIND WAYS to endow *facts* with *meanings:* give your memory more "fiber" to work on.

• For family birthdays and similar dates, use elementary astrology to endow those *dates* with *meanings.*

• Use the "divination in reverse" technique given in Chapter 6 to vitalize the astrological symbols for friends and relatives. (You need the Foundation Work for this!)

Appendices
Study Points

A

Sometimes it is necessary to "turn off" a particular program of Creative Visualization — as when a specific goal has been attained, or when a surplus of what was desired can be detrimental.

In these situations, the visualized image must be destroyed and re-absorbed.

B

For people to communicate ideas, it is valuable to use Creative Relaxation to align the various levels — physical, instinctual, emotional, intellectual and spiritual — so that it is the WHOLE PERSON who speaks the message. Thus, communication can be Mind to Mind, Emotion to Emotion, physical presence to physical presence, etc., all illuminated by the Light of the Higher Self.

C

You have a natural right to use Creative Visualization to satisfy your needs — for you are providing for yourself entirely by the development of your own natural faculties, and harming no one. With conscious knowledge of the principles of Creative Visualization, you avoid unconsciously manipulating the course of events through negative emotions. But it is only by working with, and in, the Power of the Higher Self that lasting results can be attained.

Appendix A

Terminating a Creative Visualization Process

The question has to be taken up, how to STOP a process of Creative Visualization when you have received sufficient of a particular benefit. Everyone knows the experience of the "Sorcerer's Apprentice" who enchanted a broom to bring buckets of water but had no idea how to stop the flood when there was water enough. There is another old tale of a serving-boy who found that his master had a marvelous mill, which would turn when commanded and would produce not only coffee or pepper but gold, fine fabrics or anything else that might be named. One day at dinner-time the boy, having suddenly realized there was no salt, commanded the mill, with the appropriate words, to produce it. When the house was half full of salt, he rushed out with the non-stop mill and flung it into the sea—where it goes on even now producing salt.

All the stories of magical mills, lamps, purses, or cauldrons of plenty, are images of the limitless abundance which will flow to us from the Higher Self if we make ourselves a channel for it. Why, then, should we ever want it to stop?

The cause of the trouble, if trouble there be, is this. It is the emotional-instinctual self, not the rational self, which conditions what comes from the Plenty of the Universe. The rational, conscious mind makes a decision as to what is needed and how much of it. If the emotional-instinctual self "gets the message," all is well. But it may through some secret fear or other motivation go on conditioning what is received *as it wishes,* not as the rational mind decides.

Your emotional-instinctual self can be very much like King Midas in the old legends. One legend says this king had the ears of a donkey, which shows him to represent the lower, instinctual nature. Another legend tells how he wished that *everything* he touched might turn to gold, with the result that he starved to death amid golden plates of golden food.

The lower nature CAN make mistakes of that kind. Remember the antlers of the Irish Elk! (Chapter 3)

Of course you will receive nothing but good if your emotional-instinctual self is conditioned to an ongoing desire for good health, happiness, general prosperity and success. More specific desires, however, can go on being fulfilled to a point where they are no longer helpful, but the reverse.

A shy young man may wish for the power to attract girls without the necessity to approach them first. This may be altogether to his good at the time; but if girls go on crowding round him even after he is married and the father of a young family, the situation can become distressing for all concerned. That has been known to happen in real life, in several instances.

The following is an example of over-abundance of a more literal sort. (The French even have a name for it: *embarras de richesses.*)

A young woman who was unhappily married turned as some people do to money-making for consolation. In this she had several advantages. Not only did she have considerably developed psychic abilities; her ordinary intelligence was high, and in her single days she had been secretary to the chairman of the financial committee of a large corporation. She thereby had more knowledge of how to pursue her new hobby than most girls would have had. She learned the principles of Creative Visualization, and, feeling that in this way she was being specially guided and guarded, over a number of years she built up an impressive capital.

In her middle years, having made more than enough money to meet her needs comfortably through a ripe old age, she decided to retire from financial activities. To her grief, family deaths and disputes brought her more capital still, which she could well have done without. She bought herself an historic little house with a good piece of ground in the unspoiled country, had it put in order and modernized without changing its antique charm, and looked forward to spending the rest of her days in the quiet rural locality she had chosen. She joined at first in the mild social life of her new neighbors, but soon became strangely and uncomfortably conspicuous for one thing:— almost every local lottery she entered, for no matter what good cause, brought her a substantial prize. She gave the prizes back to be re-offered, but the damage was done.

When an Air Force camp was established some miles away, it gave her a new interest without seeming to threaten her own quiet existence. She was less pleased after a few years however, when a high-grade road was built, running near her property, to link the rapidly-growing camp with the nearest large town. Soon afterwards, she saw that the land bordering the new road was bought by speculators; houses and stores were built, then factories, and the whole character of the area was swiftly changing. She went to see the planning authorities, explained her position, and was frankly congratulated by them on the growing value of her land. At the last she had neither relatives nor friends, not even a peaceful solitude; only the ever-increasing financial assets which no longer interested her. She sold up, and went into an expensive nursing home.

What had gone wrong in her life? Instead of seeing money as a means to good things, a symbol of the life-force, she had taken it as *a substitute for love.*

THIS IT CANNOT BE. THERE IS NO SUBSTI-
TUTE FOR LOVE.

Fortunately, nobody *needs* a substitute for love.
Even the most solitary person can be, and ought to be,
aware of the give-and-take of Divine Love. Towards
external beings, human or not, corporeal or not, our
need to give love is always greater than our need to
receive it. For in fact, the more love we give to any
beings whatsoever, the more Divine Love will flow from
the Higher Self into our lives in return. *But if we make
any other gratification a substitute for love, then,
because it is wholly UNSATISFYING, more and more
of that substitute we shall crave.* This is true, whether
that substitute be money or goods, food or drink, fame
or even sex.

For this reason the woman we have been telling
about, although she wearied of making money and saw
in middle life that it could help her no further, was still
unable to put through to her emotional-instinctual self
the message to stop. It persisted in its habitual program
even though this was no longer of benefit to her, and so
it became destructive, as happened in legend to King
Midas and in prehistory to the Irish Elk.

Madame David-Neil, the famous traveler whose
mystical knowledge has become a memorial to those
Tibetan Buddhist monks from whom she learned it, once
in the course of her practical studies with them fashioned
from astral substance the full-size form of a monk. At

first this artificial entity had the benign nature and appearance with which she endowed it, but after a relatively short while it became sinister and menacing. Madame David-Neil was informed that such entities usually tend to become malevolent if left to themselves, and so, under advice, she disintegrated it and re-absorbed the astral substance.

There are, clearly, more factors in that incident than can have place in this book. In one way, however, it provides a close parallel to the matters we are here considering: in Madame David-Neil's account, a visualized image which has been created and animated for good purpose, when no longer actively used goes out of control and does, or at least threatens, harm to its creator. The remedy is to disintegrate it and to re-absorb the substance.

This is exactly the case with an image formed in Creative Visualization, except that usually when such an image is no longer wanted it will just fade out: the emotional-instinctual nature will drop it in order to take up a new image proposed to it by the rational mind. But if the rational mind does not provide a new attraction, or at least not a strong enough attraction to draw the unconscious levels away from an emotional attitude of, perhaps, many years' standing, then stronger measures may be needed.

The method to be used if there is any reason for doubt is very simple and direct.

The image to be given up is brought into visualization. It is circled with a white line as in creative operations, BUT IT IS NOT CHARGED. Then, by an act of will, the image is disintegrated, broken into fragments, crumbled into a shapeless mass; and this mass is DRAWN BACK IN through that same central point of the forehead at which visualized images are created. When drawn back, it merges into you like water into the ocean. (N.B. This destruction of a purely astral image created by, and re-absorbed by, the psyche, cannot result in harm to any living being or material object.)

This method, for the purpose for which it is given, does not need illustrating by example. It is also effective, however, for any simple astral form which may be afflicting a person; and an example of this sort follows. It shows how words and actions should be adapted to a specific purpose.

A girl had a spiteful and envious cousin, some years her senior, who in order to frighten her laid claim to supranormal powers, and quite likely did try to "put a curse" on her. On growing into a pretty teenager, the girl developed a nervous affliction which interfered seriously with her daily life. She felt sure this was a result of her cousin's curse, and when she was asked why, she replied "Because every time I close my eyes I can see her staring at me!"

She was helped to realize that every person is in

essential nature both lovable and loving. The cousin, deluded by negative emotions, had created for herself a semblance of hatefulness, and had by-passed the younger girl's defensive aura by getting her to re-create this semblance *within her own psyche*. What the girl had to do now was to exteriorize this semblance by visualizing it, and then to say aloud, "This is not my cousin, who is really a lovable and loving person. This is a false likeness, and I now destroy it utterly." She then in visualization disintegrated the form, re-absorbed it in acknowledgment of the fact that it was really only a part of her own astral being, and concluded by invoking a blessing upon her cousin.

A repetition was needed before her Lower Self was truly freed from a fear which had existed from childhood, but the second performance was entirely successful and the nervous condition disappeared.

Appendix B

Helping Others
See Your Vision

You want other people to know something you know, to have faith in something you have faith in, to understand something you understand, to see something you see; and you want them *to act upon* that knowledge, that faith, that understanding, that vision.

You want this to be your regular standard of achievement, not just a once-ever miracle.

YOU CAN HAVE THIS. Let us begin at the beginnin.

If you are a teacher, preacher, politician, attorney; if you are a lecturer, demonstrator, salesman, or anyone else who has continually to set before others a view of life as a whole, or of particular facets of life,which have to be MADE REAL for those people—then FREQUENT CREATIVE RELAXATION IS A "MUST" FOR YOU.

If you are not in any of these professions, you should still READ ON! You may need this knowledge to help you win the appreciation you deserve in your job, or to help you show your children why the standards you set before them are worthwhile, or in many other life-situations. But this appendix is addressed more especially to the professional people, because so valuable an instrument as Creative Relaxation has much to offer for their particular problems of communication.

So how do you put your ideas over ALIVE?

You need frequent Creative Relaxation, NOT simply so you will have the benefit of going over your material in that final fully-relaxed part of each session! You would be well-advised to have some sessions of Creative Relaxation (at least one per week, *more* if you can) WITH NO MENTAL OR IMAGINATIVE ACTIVITY OUTSIDE OF VISUALIZING AND WELL-WISHING THE FUNCTION OF EACH PART OF YOUR BODY.

Before we consider what you want to do, we have to consider the fortifying, energizing and *unifying* effect of this powerful practice upon YOU AS A PERSON.

A Message-bearer must not intrude between the message and the recipient; but, paradoxically, if a Message-bearer is at all *negative*, that is just what will happen!

This point can be illustrated by an extreme case. A young man with high commendations for character was being trained for a position of trust in a government department. One day, quite incidentally to his work, he was told to hand a moderate sum of money to a certain official whom (as it happened) he had not yet met.

He found this official talking on the telephone; and being doubtful what to do, he hesitated, tried to catch the man's eye, thought he had succeeded, put the money down on the desk and hurried back to his post. Later, inquiries were made about the money. Maybe the official had absent-mindedly put it away and forgotten it, maybe it had gotten covered over or maybe someone else removed it, but nobody who was asked could say where it was and when the young trainee stated the official had *seen* him put it on the desk, this was not confirmed either.

No accusation could be made against the trainee, but he was soon removed to another sphere of usefulness. *What fault had he in fact manifested?* Diffidence, negativeness. HE HAD NOT "PUT OVER" HIS MESSAGE.

YOU, of course, have learned how to communicate. You have been trained to express yourself lucidly, forcefully, persuasively. *How far does that take you?*

Many people spend a high proportion of their free time *being entertained by* other people expressing themselves lucidly, forcefully, persuasively. And year by year people develop a higher resistance to taking in what they see or hear.

YOU MAY BE A TRAINED SPEAKER BUT UNLESS YOU ARE AT A UNIVERSITY YOU PROBABLY DON'T HAVE MANY TRAINED LISTENERS: AND IF YOU ARE AT A UNIVERSITY THE COMPETITION FOR THOSE TRAINED LISTENERS' ATTENTION IS ACUTE.

That is why you need Creative Relaxation to align the various levels of yourself — your physical, instinctual, emotional, intellectual and spiritual levels — so that YOU as a whole person give reality to your message.

If your message is to be positive, YOU must be positive.
If your message is to be dynamic, YOU must be dynamic.

That much, you will realize, is only a beginning in your task. BUT IT IS A NECESSARY BEGINNING.

As a message-bearer, you need health, energy, magnetism. Anything cold or standoffish in you COULD BE FELT AS SOMETHING STANDOFFISH IN YOUR MESSAGE!

This is particularly important in these days when so many people are apt, as we have suggested, through sheer jaded weariness of the often futile demands they daily experience, to *close the doors* of mind and brain against rational argument, even against plain evidence. But the doors of the instincts, the emotions, the unconscious perceptions *cannot so easily be closed.*

What follows contains some salient considerations on the *mechanism and ethics of using this method of persuasion.*

You want your rational argument to be rationally accepted. You want your hearers to be happy that they have rationally considered and accepted what you put to them.

BUT IT CAN BE RATIONALLY ACCEPTED ONLY WHEN IT HAS BEEN GIVEN A FAIR HEARING. *How will you ensure its being given a fair hearing?*

BY THE APPEAL OF YOUR ALIGNED INSTINCTS, EMOTIONS, UNCONSCIOUS PERCEPTIONS, WITH YOUR RATIONAL MIND AND PHYSICAL PRESENCE — OF YOU AS A TOTAL PERSON — TO THE TOTAL PERSON OF YOUR HEARERS, MIND TO MIND, EMOTIONAL NATURE TO EMOTIONAL NATURE, PHYSICAL PRESENCE TO PHYSICAL PRESENCE, AND THE REST.

YOUR MESSAGE WILL ALSO BE ACTIVATED BY THE LIGHT OF YOUR HIGHER SELF.

So powerful is the battery of persuasion that we have here proposed, that the question of its ethical justification will at once occur to you.

We too have had to be sure of this justification, in deciding to place this most potent instrument of persuasion in the hands of the public. To have put forth a book on Creative Visualization without the present chapter would still have been to give the necessary knowledge implicitly, but this chapter makes it explicit.

The few writers who have ever dealt with subjects of this nature have either known so little themselves that it didn't matter, or else have tried to justify themselves by giving part of their information in hints, riddles and dead languages; as if a talent for ferreting out facts, reading Latin and Greek, or cracking ciphers were limited to the scrupulous.

That is not the way these great powers are safeguarded!

In the first place, let it be clearly stated that you are not justified in trying to *over-persuade* anyone to make any purchase, join any organization, or to assent to any opinion. In other words, if he has given your case a fair hearing and his considered opinion is still against it, you may if time and circumstances warrant it go on trying to convince him, but you must not in the mean-time try to get him to speak or act at variance with his opinion.

This rule is, very often, simply a special instance of the rule given earlier in this book for successful Creative Visualization, that *you should not specify a material source of supply.*

To illustrate this, take the example of a salesman who, in Creative Visualization, has set a high target for his commission. This is in itself a very valid thing to do. He is also right, having visualized for that target, to work his best for the sales to reach it. HE IS NOT ENTITLED HOWEVER TO FIX ON ANY ONE PERSON AS A CUSTOMER.

The person may have excellent reasons for not buying at this time.

A girl who was accustomed to spending plenty of money on her clothes, one day had bad news from her people. Considerable economizing would be necessary.

She was at first a great deal depressed by the thought of this; and besides, she needed a new dress. She knew nothing of Creative Visualization, but being a resourceful person she decided to cheer herself up by going to one of the very good and expensive stores she favored. She could enjoy the luxurious atmosphere as usual, she could at any rate have a cup of coffee there, and she could try on some dresses. That way, she would find what looked best on her among the new fashions, and could seek out the nearest article to it at a less expensive store in another district, perhaps a few weeks later. At the store she was going to now, she was not usually pressed to buy immediately.

This time, however, no sooner was she looking at a row of dresses than a young sales clerk approached her and evidently wanted to rush a purchase. The girl who had only come to look replied that she was not buying at once; she wanted to get an idea what was available, because soon she would be buying a new coat and would then choose a dress to go with it.

"Our new season's coats are just in," said the clerk, "do come this way and take a look, they really are beautiful!" Having glanced at the visitor's own clothes, she expected some extravagant purchases to be made, and a fat commission for herself.

So pressing was she that before long the girl who really would hardly have dared at the time to buy a scarf at that store, found herself wearing an expensive afternoon dress pinned about her for a trimmer fit at the waist, a sumptuous coat, elegant shoes, a hat, purse, scarf and gloves to complete the outfit. "Just see how good it looks on you," purred the clerk.

"I *can't* buy anything today. I only meant to look around, and I didn't bring my checkbook," protested the victim who was now rather alarmed. The clerk thought of the expensive labels she'd noticed on the other's things in the dressing-room, and made a quick decision. "Come through here, please," she whispered.

Behind a screen was a small table with writing materials. From a locked drawer the clerk produced a book of blank checks. "Which is your bank?" she asked.

The visitor saw no escape but in flight. "It's so hot in here, I feel sick — must have air!" she cried. She dashed into the dressing-room, snatched off the gloves, the scarf, the hat, the coat, slipped into her own coat, picked up her purse in place of the loaned one, and fled. The clerk stared. It took her some time to realize she had a good but worn dress and pair of shoes in place of the ones the visitor had been over-persuaded to try on. She could but report the matter to her supervisor, but the "shoplifter" never reappeared, being too thoroughly scared even to return the things.

That, too, is a true story! "Nothing like it could happen in the business world, in the world of spiritual or intellectual thought?" Worse happens. Bankruptcies and suicides have followed over-persuaded signatures; lifetimes of perplexity have followed a "false start" in life for people who have accepted a choice which was not theirs in religion or in study.

Knowing this, how can we give to EVERYONE the knowledge of this powerful means of persuasion?

The answer is simple. We admit that harm can be done, for a time, by merely astral image-building by the greedy or the misguided. This, unfortunately, happens ceaselessly, whether people understand the principles or not. *But the incentive to depend knowingly on such methods is very slight.* People who apply undue or unworthy pressures through astral image-building may benefit in money or in prestige for a time, or they may not. They have continually to take their chances. The spiritual world does not guarantee them their gain, and the reverse which overtakes them is often swift, unexpected and final.

You can only effectively CALL UPON your Higher Self to give lastingness to what you win, if your gain of it is in accord with your own conscience. As we have said in Chapter 5, *your conscience is part of your Lower Self, but it has the power to close the door to communication with your Higher Self.* And we know how completely it does so for people who misuse such methods as we are giving here.

We can leave, therefore, these somewhat negative aspects of the matter, and go forward with our positive, inspiring and radiant theme.

YOU ARE CONVINCED THAT YOU ARE ABLE, WHETHER BY SPIRITUAL, INTELLECTUAL OR MATERIAL BENEFITS, TO BRING AN INCREASED MEASURE OF HAPPINESS AND FULFILLMENT INTO THE LIVES OF OTHERS. Your own well-being is probably also involved in your doing so. This is a just condition, which applies in many walks of life.

What is necessary for this state of things to bring real benefits to those others as well as to yourself, is that THEY SHOULD BE ABLE TO SEE AND TO APPRE-CIATE THE BENEFITS YOU CAN BRING TO THEM, AS YOU SEE AND APPRECIATE THOSE BENEFITS.

You have made yourself into an effective Message-bearer by frequent Creative Relaxation. Now you have to formulate and energize the matter of the message itself; *also by sessions of Creative Relaxation if you wish, or by sessions of Creative Visualization should you feel it is better to make that distinction.*

If you perform this in Creative Relaxation, the activity will naturally be in the final, fully-relaxed stage of the session; it will, essentially, be the same as if you use the seated position. *In either position, TAKE ESPECIAL CARE TO MAINTAIN THE RHYTHMIC BREATH.* This has great effect in linking the astral and material levels.

Helping others see your vision

Go over, systematically, in your mind, as if you were speaking to someone, the most attractive, telling and advantageous points that you will want to bring to people's attention.

Now visualize a picture of YOUR VISION the way you want people to see it. Never mind if as you see it now it seems rather over-colored or intense. *You have to work with your emotional nature in order to reach other people's emotional nature, and that is quite a different thing from the work of the rational mind.*

BE MOVED BY WHAT YOU VISUALIZE. DON'T BE AFRAID OR ASHAMED TO BE MOVED BY WHAT YOU VISUALIZE. Be enthusiastic about it, excited about it. Be AWARE how much good it can do, how much good it WILL DO. See in it all those good features you have just enumerated mentally.

Imagine other people — a man, a woman, men and women collectively BUT NOT SPECIFIC PERSONS — standing beside you. You are showing them your vision, they see all the goodness in it. They KNOW this is true!

Ring the main object of your vision with a white line. Now, using your favorite method of those given in Chapter 4, fill yourself with the Light of your Higher Self and charge the ringed image so that it is radiant to the boundary of the white circle. Keep your imagined people there gazing at it with you. *See it as altogether splendid, desirable, satisfying.* If you can express this in a brief audible phrase, do so! Then let the picture fade slowly from visualization.

When you have done this effectively several times, *you will have formed a definite image in the astral world.* (So don't vary it!) You will also have impressed the same image very clearly in your own astral body, and thus in your own emotional nature. You have not only CREATED this picture in the astral world, you have definitely established your own link with it.

By infusing this image with the Light of your Higher Self, you have given it a lasting quality so that it will not drift and change as merely astral pictures sometimes do. Any person with a developed faculty of clairvoyance would immediately see this image as a real astral object or scene (which it is, now) and would sense the good qualities with which you have associated that vision.

Clairvoyance, however, is but a special perception of *what is.* YOUR ASTRAL CREATION IS JUST AS REALLY THERE FOR A PERSON WHO CAN'T SEE IT CLAIRVOYANTLY, AS FOR ONE WHO CAN.

(Make no mistake about this; it does sometimes confuse people. If two men go into a dark room where there is a table, and one man can see in the dark while the other can't, the table is just as really there for the man who can't see it and he will probably prove this by walking into it!)

Furthermore, by the "reciprocal" image in your own psyche, you are keeping a hold on the astral reality rather like holding a kite by means of a twine.

Afterwards, whenever you are talking to people on this subject (whether one person or many, but treating all alike) DON'T TALK ABOUT IT IN THE ABSTRACT! Make it THAT VISION you are telling them about, that vision which you have seen and which you want to enable them to see. You don't always have to use the same words about it, but bring in some at least of the phrases you have associated with it. Describe it. Feel sure you are enabling them to see it, making it *their vision too*. THIS WILL WORK.

DO NORMAL CREATIVE VISUALIZATION DAILY FOR RESULTS TOO! For instance, a salesman could set himself a target in money and visualize for it daily: while a weekly "Vision" practice on what he sells will add zest to his work, for himself as well as for his customers.

Here an important distinction can usefully be made. The salesman TALKS ABOUT the subject of his "Vision" work; *that is its chief purpose!* He DOES NOT TALK ABOUT his private Creative Visualization: he doesn't go around saying "I'm going to sell five more of these cars in record time and then I shall buy a house!" Such a thing would be bad visualization practice anyway — and if a customer heard it, it would be plain bad psychology!

BESIDES THESE TWO SEPARATE PRACTICES, FURTHERMORE, DON'T FORGET AT LEAST ONCE A WEEK, CREATIVE RELAXATION WITHOUT "VISION WORK," FOR YOUR OWN PSYCHO-PHYSICAL GOOD!

Appendix C

The Bright Lamp
of Knowledge

Wisdom is simply Wisdom.

It may appear as Eastern or Western, as connected with this or that creed or philosophy when we consider the images, the words, the doctrines which are peripheral to its utterances. The essentials of those utterances, however, stand beyond and clear of all such limitations. That is why, in any tradition which is not specifically a "wisdom tradition," the wise are often regarded as somewhat suspect by people who are more carefully orthodox.

For the same reason, the spiritual truth contained in such utterances *overflows its context*. It is always good to understand the purpose to which a wisdom utterance was originally directed; but by its nature, it involves a spiritual perception which far exceeds that purpose.

The wisdom texts which we can relate to Creative Visualization do not, usually, present anything like a complete picture. In some cases the teachers may not themselves have been aware of the complete picture; in many cases what we have are the utterances of advanced mystics who no longer cared at all for the possibility of material realization; in other cases again there has been an active desire on the part of the teachers TO AVOID MAKING PUBLIC THE PRINCIPLES AND PRACTICE OF CREATIVE VISUALIZATION.

It is our opinion that this secrecy should not be continued, for three reasons:

(1) Many people have need of material goods or of inner development, which they can obtain by Creative Visualization but would not expect as an ordinary event.

In using Creative Visualization, these people are providing for themselves ENTIRELY BY THE DEVELOPMENT AND USE OF THEIR OWN NATURAL FACULTIES, as each individual has a natural right to do.

(2) Spiritual force is coming into material manifestation (and going out of it) continually, whether any human agency takes conscious part in the operation or not.

We also see human beings frequently causing disaster for themselves or for others, by *unconsciously* manipulating the course of events through negative emotions. *It would be better for all to understand this.*

(3) *ONLY BY WORKING WITH, AND IN, THE POWER OF THE HIGHER SELF CAN LASTING RESULTS BE ASSURED.*

Our purpose, therefore, is to put together in the present appendix a number of texts, both those already quoted in this book and others, which show, in the words of mystical writers of diverse traditions, *either* the spiritual truths underlying Creative Visualization, *or* the effects of the positive application of those truths, whether or not this is wrought specifically by visualization.

The first quotation is from *Black Elk Speaks; being the Life Story of a Holy Man of the Oglala Sioux, as told to John G. Neihardt.* * (There are several passages in which Black Elk's words imply the same spiritual background that is stated here, but this one is particularly succinct and explicit.)

"Crazy Horse dreamed and went into the world where there is nothing but the spirits of all things. That is the real world that is behind this one, and everything we see here is like a shadow from that world . . . It was this vision that gave him his great power . . . "

Elsewhere in that book, John G. Neihardt has a footnote stating that Black Elk could not read and had no knowledge of world affairs. Our next quotation is from Plotinus (born in Egypt around 205 C.E.).

"The greatness of Intelligence may be seen also in the following way. We admire the magnitude and beauty of the sense world, the eternal regularity of its movements,

*Pocket Books (New York) 1973.

its visible and invisible living beings, its earth-spirits, animals and plants. Let us then rise to its model, the superior reality from which this world derives, and there contemplate the whole array of intelligibles which eternally possess their inalienable intelligence and life. Over there preside pure Intelligence and incredible Wisdom." (*Plotinus, Ennead V.1, adapted from the translation by Joseph Katz.**)

The *Ratnamegha Sutra,* a document of Mahayana Buddhism, tells us the following about the bodhisatva. (A bodhisatva is an enlightened being who does not accept the bliss of Buddhahood, returning to aid mankind.)

"The bodhisatva, thoroughly examining the nature of things, dwells in ever-present mindfulness of the activity of mind; and so does not fall into the mind's control, but the mind comes under his control. And with the mind under his control, all phenomena are under his control."

Many of the texts of Buddhism, because of their intellectual mode of approaching their subject, are apt to make Buddhism seem cold to those who only know it from the outside. In fact, no way of life which can lead to enlightenment is cold. However, there is a change in tempo when we turn to the song of a Persian mystic, who is describing the sure way to the sublime goal.

*Appleton-Century-Crofts (1950).

Although his statement is limpidly straightforward, he evidently does not mean its sense to be minimized. Its promise should be taken literally, but the cup is deeper than it seems!

The Terdjih Bend was written in the 18th century C.E. by Ahmed Hatif; our quotation is from the Aurum Solis version which is given in Volume V of *The Magical Philosophy:*

> "When all things that you see,
> see you with love,
> Then all things that you love
> soon will you see."

Scholars have for centuries been debating the rival dignities of Love and Knowledge, but the mystic knows that in matters divine the debate is without purpose, for the two are inseparable. The medieval Hindu musician-saint, *Pey of Mylapore,* has this:

"Lighting in my heart the bright lamp of knowledge, I sought and captured Him: softly the Lord of Miracles entered my heart and stayed there without leaving."

From the New Testament, these are basic:

"The kingdom of God is within you." *(Luke chapter 17, v.21)*

"But seek ye first the kingdom of God and his righteousness, and all these things [food, drink, clothing] shall be added unto you." *(Matthew chapter 6, verse 23)*

This could be called *The Gospel of Plenty:*

"Ask, and it shall be given you; seek, and ye shall find; knock, and it shall be opened unto you. For every one that asketh, receiveth; and he that seeketh findeth; and to him that knocketh it shall be opened. Or what man is there of you, whom if his son ask bread, will give him a stone? Or if he ask a fish, will he give him a serpent? If ye then, being evil, know how to give good gifts to your children, how much more shall your Father which is in heaven give good things to them that ask him? Therefore all things whatsoever ye would that men should do to you, do ye even so to them: for this is the law and the prophets." *(Matthew chapter 7, v. 7 through 12)*

There are other passages which could be quoted (some of which are given in Chapter 4) tracing our themes like a thread through the complex tapestry of the New Testament; but these two will suffice here:

"If you have faith as a grain of mustard seed, ye shall say unto this mountain, Remove hence to yonder place, and it shall remove; and nothing shall be impossible to you." *(Matthew chapter 18, v.20)*

"Give, and it shall be given unto you: good measure, pressed down, and shaken together, and running over, shall men give into your bosom. For with the same measure that ye mete withal it shall be measured to you again." *(Luke chapter 7, v.38)*

The foregoing is the background to *John Wesley's* well-known piece of advice:

"Get all you can. Give all you can."

Going back to the power of the visual imagination over material phenomena, we refer again to *Dr. O. Carl Simonton* whose account is quoted rather more fully on page 128 , of the psychic activity observed in a number of unexpectedly improving patients:

". . . the important thing was what they pictured and the way they saw things. They were positive, regardless of the source, and their picture was very positive."

(Although many histories exist, a number of which have been given in this book, of the power of the visual imagination which is, indeed, an accepted fact to mystics and occultists, yet the research and evidence of this medical doctor, involving the disappearance of serious disease symptoms from the seers themselves, appears to us to be superlatively worth giving again.)

Finally, in connection with the inner power of Visualization, must be mentioned also that of Affirmation — Mantram — Song. The strong counsel of King Alfred the Great, therefore, is given the last word:

"If you have a fearful thought,
To a weakling tell it not:
To your saddle-pommel breathe it,
   And ride forth singing!

Appendix D

Creative Visualization in Prayer and Worship

The use of Creative Visualization in prayer and worship probably comes more easily, in many cases, to the followers of a religion which has a great deal of ready made sacred imagery, than it does to people of a more austere and imageless faith. None the less, to possess religious faith is so great an advantage in developing the inner life that, even with a religion which lacks any specific imagery of its own, the believer has a head-start over the materialist in the matter of Creative Visualization.

To be sure, not all believers worship, and not all believers pray. To these people, however, some of the ideas which follow may appeal; they may then wish to think of, or even to picture, the Deity they themselves believe in. When that is done, the step to worship and to prayer is more imaginable.

"But how shall I pray? How shall I ever begin

praying?" some may ask. You might begin as children begin speaking, with a single word; some of the world's greatest and most powerful prayers have been just a single word. For the rest, there is no "how", no "proper form of address". Nothing is more intimate, more unique than the relationship between Deity and worshiper: whether you say something which nobody has ever said in worship before, or whether you use the same words as a hundred thousand other devotees, is of no importance. *What matters is that these words are your prayer now;* and you will have found one of the greatest sources of strength, of inspiration, of spiritual insight, of joy and confidence at every level of being, that have been known to humanity in all lands and through all ages.

With regard to visualization, it is not suggested that anyone should overpass any doubts they hold as to the rightness—or the possibility—of imagining Deity in any localized form. At the same time, if you wish to increase the benefits you can gain by using Creative Visualization in your worship and prayer, you should consider whether there is *some* spiritual Being you can hold in your visual imagination, either as recipient or as carrier of your petitions to Deity.

For those who can worship their God or Goddess in a traditional symbolic form, or for worshipers of an incarnated Deity, no further counsel may be needed as to the Divine Being they should visualize. If you have any difficulty in this matter, however, you might be happy to picture your Guardian Angel, or a Saint, and ask that Being to present your prayers and petitions to Deity. (Your Saint may be a recognized Saint whose name you bear, like Martha or Barbara, John or Patrick for instance, or one associated with the subject of your current visualization project.* Or he or she may be a person not recognized as a Saint by any church: any person who has passed over and whom you love and venerate—a grandparent perhaps— would be appropriate here. As early missionaries to China soon found, "ancestor worship" and veneration of the Saints are, at root, much the same thing!

You can, of course, visualize both your Deity and a holy helper; many people do this and it is very powerful.

Whether you are visualizing Deity in any form, or an Angel or Saint, take care to "see" that Being in as gracious and benign an aspect as you can: radiant, powerful, welcoming and compassionate. If you can obtain, or make, a picture or sculpture of this likeness, it will probably help your visualization. *But remember, you are not expected to attribute any power to the material image itself,* you are not making either a fetish or a talisman of it. It is just meant to aid you in formulating as clearly as possible your inward visualized image, and also to avoid for you the difficulty of praying "into space" with conviction.

A Hindu devotee once described how, in prayer, he offered lights and flowers with words of love and adoration

---

*The guardianship of special areas of earthly wants and needs by special Saints is a most fascinating and rewarding study. It will be the subject of a future book on the Saints, the Tarot, and Creative Visualization.

to the likeness of his Deity. "But when my time of worship is ended," he said, "I leave the stone image upon the altar and put the true image back within my heart."

The more strongly you can build up the "true image within your heart", the better it will avail you. For this reason you should make a firm practice of your devotions for some considerable time before you ask for anything by this method. Admittedly, if it is some serious emergency which has prompted you to try prayer, this initial practice of worship may not be possible.

Emergencies occur in which people pray who never prayed before, and in which people pray to Powers they never addressed before; and frequently these petitioners receive what they ask. *But in emergencies you have access to areas of your Deep Mind which are sealed from you in more normal circumstances; and to be able to pray effectively when there is no crisis is something you cannot count on without practice.*

If you enter upon the Way of Devotion therefore, follow it with perseverance and with all the fervor you can find within yourself.

Set up a small altar, or a "special corner" for your worship. You can pray standing, sitting, kneeling or in any posture you choose; several traditional modes of worship include a whole series of postures. If possible, make a habit of lighting a lamp or burning candles to accompany your period of prayer. Flowers or incense may also grace your altar if you feel them to be appropriate. *But in any case, when you pray, visualize.* That is essential.

If you think of God as Light, then visualize Light. If to you the Divine Presence would be something almost palpable on a mountain top, or in a cavern, then visualize that you are on a mountain top or in a cavern before you begin praying.

When you have an objective you wish to gain through this mode of prayer, the basic principles are the same whether you are to address an intermediary Being, or Deity directly. However, the details of procedure differ somewhat in the different cases, so they are listed separately below:

A.   If you are going to visualize, in whatever manner, the Deity to who you pray—*and no intermediary Being—*proceed as follows:

(1)   Build up first a clear visualized image of the objective you seek: whether it is a benefit for soul or body, whether it is for yourself or for another. Formulate a distinct picture: the person restored to health for instance, or the certificate for passing an examination being handed to you. Or, if the objective you seek is something visible and material, then simply formulate a picture of the thing itself, preferably "seeing" it being used by its intended owner whether yourself or another.

(2)   Visualize your image of Deity, whether in human or other shape or simply as Light, shining and beneficent.

(3)   Make adoration of the Deity, in terms such as

you usually use in your prayers or such as you feel moved to use now.

(4)   State, clearly and precisely, what you want. State without hesitation that this is *needed;* don't shrink from being emotional about this, if you feel so inclined.

(5)   "See" that which you desire made radiant by Divine contact, and given to you by the Deity; or "hear"— and repeat over to yourself—the words which tell you the event *will come to pass.* Accept the gift, and give thanks for it.

(6)   Let all that you have visualized fade gently from your consciousness.

(7)   During the day, and during the night if you awaken, recall the action described in (5)—if only for a moment at a time—and again give thanks.

(8)   When that for which you have prayed really comes to pass in the material world, *don't fail to give special thanks for it.* And continue in your devotions with renewed faith.

B.   If you are making your request with the aid of an intermediary, a holy helper—*whether you are also going to visualize a Divine presence or no*—then proceed in the manner following:

(1)   As (1) above.

(2)   Visualize your chosen intermediary, the holy person or angelic Being with whom you have a particular relationship or who is specially concerned with the subject-matter of your request.

(3)   Make a sincere and fitting greeting to this Being.

Then ask this Being to carry your request *(which at this point you do not state in detail)* to the Deity *(whom you name, or denote by an acceptable title)*. Ask your intermediary to intercede for you *(and for anyone else whom the request concerns)* and to obtain for you *(and for the other person)* what is needed. BE POSITIVE THAT WHAT YOU ASK WILL BE DONE.

(4)   Visualize your intermediary going to present your request to the Deity; really *going:* walking, flying, what you will. Whether or not you intend to visualize the Deity, take care to "see" your intermediary taking your request. This is a very potent part of the procedure.

(5)   If you intend to visualize your Deity, do so now. *In any case,* center your attention on the Deity and make your salutation and adoration, addressing the Deity directly.

(6)   State, clearly and precisely, what you seek. State without hesitation that this is *needed;* don't be afraid to be emotional about this, if you feel like it. Remember also to state that your holy helper *(whom you name)* is asking this along with you.

(7)   Turning your attention from the Divine presence, "see" your intermediary coming back to you, glad and radiant, with your request granted. "See" the object being given to you, or "hear" the words which tell you that the event *will come to pass.* Accept the gift, and give thanks for it.

(8)   Let all you have visualized fade gently from your consciousness.

(9)   During the day, and during the night if you

awaken, recall the action described in (7)—if only for a
moment at a time—and again give thanks.

(10)   When that for which you have prayed really
comes to pass in the material world, *don't fail to give
special thanks for it*. Continue in your devotions with
strengthened faith—and don't forget your holy helper.

In the Way of Devotion, care should be taken about
one point. Whatever you are seeking in this way, *seek in
this way only*: that is, so far as spiritual means are
concerned. Of course if you are sick, take normal earthly
means to be cured as well as praying for healing; and if
you want to pass an exam, study for it as well as praying
about it. The real meaning here is, if you are seeking some
special thing by a devotional procedure as outlined above,
you should not attempt "spiritual insurance" which goes
outside the system. If you are asking a vital boon from the
Queen of Heaven, don't throw a coin in the wishing well
as a bid for the same thing.

You may explain this need for care by saying, as the
people of the Old Testament did, that your God is
"jealous". Or, if the idea of jealousy doesn't fit with your
idea of Deity, it cn be explained in another way. (Which
seems to indicate, also, why using normal material-world
means to get what you want will work along with your
prayers, not hinder them).

Your spiritual link with the Divine Power you have
invoked, your mental identification of that Power, together
with your devotional fervor and your sense of need (and

ordinary material things such as medicine, money etc.) are "neutral" and may easily be used by the Divine Power as part of the material level of that channel.

However, if you introduce other, lesser channels particularly at astral level, to that visualized image, you may easily create a leak in the system: like puncturing a drinking straw, or, worse, like puncturing a tire! In such a case, you'd be starting right back at the beginning.

Think of the many aspects of Deity; then of the clear perceptions some gifted seers and teachers hve had concerning them. Then think of the emotions and mind-pictures built up by innumerable faithful worshipers through the ages, forming the lower part of the channel of power; and you will see how some great shrines have remained living centers of faith and of miracle for centuries.

Never forget this: behind all your visualizing and image-building, giving it validity and meaning, is the reality of Deity; a more real reality than any earthly thing, a Power more powerful and more loving than we can comprehend. If we can only learn to ask aright—and a full trust and a clear perception of our real wants is what is meant here—there is no limit to the abundance, both spiritual and material, with which we shall be blessed.

Appendix E

Maintaining Good Health

In this book there is some important evidence for the value of Creative Visualization to aid recovery from sickness. Creative Visualization has another area of effective use which can be of great value to *everyone:* the maintenance of good health.

Good diet, rest, fresh air, exercise: these things all make for good health. Many people could do with more of at least one of them; but another need which is probably even more important is to get full value out of whatever good diet, rest, fresh air and exercise is within your reach: to get full value out of it mentally and emotionally as well as physically.

We not only need to have these good things; if our bodies are to derive full benefit from them, *we need to know we have them.* Most important of all, our Deep Mind needs to be made fully aware of them.

So great is the power of the imagination, that it is difficult in many instances to draw a dividing line between making full use of what we have, and thriving without something we don't have which would normally be considered essential. This question arises when people survive in conditions which would have been expected to make survival impossible, and sometimes survive without any perceptible physical or emotional damage. What stands out on examination, however, is that the survivors *expected* to survive. In conditions of food shortage, there have been people who thought of their meager supplies as sufficient to support life. Where others saw themselves as starving, *these people did not become anxious;* and they survived.

Here we are not discussing instances of total fasting. Some people, certainly, have survived long periods of total fasting; others have attempted this and speedily died. What we are looking for is the power which enables the body to derive full benefit and satisfaction from food which *is* eaten; and the evidence is that we must look for this factor, not in the body but in the mind.

This is an important factor in healthy living at the present time for, surprisingly, the problem of hunger affects those who are over-nourished as well as the under-nourished.

Many people overeat compulsively as a result of stress and anxiety. Clearly, this is not a problem of the conscious mind; for the cause of it, we must look into the workings of the emotional-instinctual nature.

From remote ages to the present, the chief cause of anxiety for most humans has been the fear of hunger, famine. The direct result of that fear (not only on humans but on any sentient creatures) is demonstrable, and is just what might be expected: when a supply of food is present, the impulse is to eat as much as possible while it lasts. This looks like an outcome of rational thinking but in fact it is quite instinctive, and is profoundly linked to the basic instinct of self-preservation.

Our Deep Mind can do some very wonderful things for us, but it is *sub-rational;* it works entirely at the instinctual level of our psycho-physical being. When we are worried or anxious about something—no matter what—if we don't make the situation very clear to our Deep Mind there is a danger that it may connect this emotion of anxiety, insecurity, fear, with the primal fear of famine. If this happens, it prompts us compulsively to eat all we can *now.*

For this reason some of the advice which compulsive eaters, anxiety eaters, need is exactly the advice they would need if they were really short of food.

Of course, where a weight problem is harming a person's health, he or she needs expert advice on losing some weight without delay. Likewise, everyone needs to have a proper and sensible diet for his or her age, height, weight, sex, type of work and state of health, and any serious or puzzling condition should receive medical attention. *Beyond all this, however, there remains one thing you can and should do for yourself,* and nobody can do it for you. Besides getting the right food, medication, exercise, whatever it may be, *you should make sure your Deep Mind knows it is right.*

Whatever your problem concerning food, therefore, and even if you have no problem at all, you would do well to adopt these suggestions:

First, make sure you are eating the food best suited to you, out of what is presently available to you. Don't distress yourself over what may not be as you would wish: resolve that what you have is going to do you good. Share this resolve with your Deep Mind by speaking it aloud, quietly but firmly.

For people of a religious outlook, "saying grace" before and/or after meals is an excellent way to bring the Deep Mind into the proceedings, provided the words used are specific enough to carry the message. The food which is now before us is viewed as the gift of the beneficent Power who guards and sustains us; in accepting this gift, we are sustained both in body and in soul. Or the Crowleyan "Will" is also a good and helpful formula: the

---

*If you want to do Creative Visualization for a supply of more or better food, or for some particular item which you need, you have two options: (1) to do your Creative Visualization for this purpose at least an hour away from eating, and preferably first thing in the morning; or (2) set out your meal, and, by way of "grace" before eating it, bless it in accordance with the Multiplication Technique (page 164); in your preliminary contemplation of the food visualizing it as including everything you wish. Then, when you have completed the Technique and allowed the Light to fade from your awareness, eat with good will and perfect confidence. The Multiplication Technique can be used very effectively in other needs besides, but it has most anciently been associated with food.

diner declares his or her will to eat and drink, that the body may be strengthened in order to accomplish the Great Work: tht is, to fulfill the person's special destiny.

Eat slowly but steadily. don't (if you can avoid it) read, watch TV, join in exciting talk or listen to radio newscasts meanwhile. As you chew each mouthful, think of the nourishment, strength and energy this food will give you. (Take care, particularly if you are overweight, NOT to let your approval of the food become focused instead on its attractive appearance, smell or flavor.)

From time to time, cast your mind over what you look forward to as a result of this good meal: benefit in work, exercise, an evening's fun, better health, better looks, sound sleep and a refreshed awakening. Visualize your muscles, nerves, hair, skin, blood being really fortified by this food.

Think, and imagine confidently, that when you've finished your quota of food you will *feel* satisfied and *be* well-nourished.

Eating slowly serves two purposes. As the doctors tell us, it makes the food more digestible and truly more satis-fying, because when well chewed it can be better dealt with by the stomach and because the process of digestion is in fact begun by the action of the saliva in the mouth. But also—another important angle—eating slowly gives your Deep Mind a chance to catch up on what you are doing, to absorb the message that this food is really adequate, nourishing, energy-giving, satisfying.

In Chapter 2, some valuable attention is given to the topic of rest and relaxation. Little needs to be added to it here. It is good, however, *at any time* when you rest—even if you are not doing a detailed Relaxation—just to check that all the main parts of your body, including your head and face, are relaxed.

A related topic which needs to be mentioned here is that of insomnia. One thing worse than insomnia itself is *worry about insomnia:* like any other worry, this is a waste of time which could be given to creative action.

Chronic insomnia needs medical care, but occasionally missing a night's sleep need trouble nobody. Besides, supposing for instance you are sleepless on account of an important day's work you have to do tomorrow?—anxiety about not sleeping now won't help you, can only make matters worse.

If any specific physical or mental cause is preventing you from sleeping, try to deal with that first. If an idea has come to you with regard to your next day's work, and you are afraid to go to sleep before fixing it in your memory, you would do much better to get up, clarify your thoughts, put your idea effectively on paper or on tape and then return to the other question, of getting to sleep.

When you are back in bed, relax thoroughly, slowly and by detailed procedure, *and stay relaxed.* Refuse to entertain any further intellectual thought; just check over your limbs and trunk from time to time to make sure they stay relaxed. Establish Rhythmic Breath (pages 43–46) and breathe deeply and steadily, as you would when sleeping. *Picture yourself as sleeping.*

Most likely you'll fall asleep; and even if you don t, you will have a better night's rest than you would have done without this relaxation.

Supposing some kind of pain keeps you awake when you either have no pain-killers or don't want to use any, and you don't know the right pressure-point to relieve it?

Simply pretending a pain doesn't exist is not only difficult, on the evidence it doesn't seem to be a good idea. Your Deep Mind's knowledge of the truth of the matter could cause the pain to be "repressed": that is, your physical and emotional-instinctual experience of it could be saved up somewhere beyond your consciousness, to be presented to you at another time which might be even less convenient.

Until a pain goes or can be relieved it needs to be "accepted"; but this does not mean dwelling on it. Fixing the attention on even a small physical discomfort can magnify it intolerably, while considerable pain can be lived with if the attention is kept on something else. Only DON'T tell your Deep Mind "I don't have a pain" or "Pain doesn't exist". That would (1) keep your attention directed in a negative way to the very topic you want to turn it away from, and (2) lose the confidence of your Deep Mind which knows you are trying to tell it something contrary to its experience.

So, here again, establish Rhythmic Breath and give your attention to a detailed relaxation. *When you come to the muscles in the painful area, take special care to relax those as much as the others.* If there is any injury, inflammation, neuralgia, visualize this as being healed, soothed, relaxed, the cause of the pain being wiped out. A good image for many people is to visualize slender, cool, gentle fingers touching or stroking the pain-spot, soothing and healing it. As you visualize this, pay attention not only to "seeing" those fingers but to "feeling" the firm, gentle touch, the distinct coolness, the healing.

Keep up the Rhythmic Breath, go on and relax the rest of your muscles. Stay relaxed as long as you can, then repeat the whole process including the visualization. You probably will fall asleep, and will awaken a great deal more refreshed than if you had simply drugged yourself into forgetfulness. In any case, you will have rested effectively and will have done a great deal to help yourself, whatever the cause of your trouble may be.

You Deep Mind is the most wonderful instrument and helper you can have. However, it has to be your instrument and helper; never your master. With all its wonderful powers, your Deep Mind—the unconscious part of your emotional-instinctual nature—is part of your Lower Self, and must never be confused with your Higher Self (page 85). Just as your rational mind should learn to be aware of, and to pay heed to, the promptings of your Higher Self, so your Deep Mind which is part of your Lower Self should be guided and led by your rational mind. Left to its own devices, your Deep Mind is quite incapable of running your life aright.

We have noted how, for example, you might be worried about your car or your promotion—or even your figure!—and your Deep Mind might totally misinterpret the anxiety and prompt you to eat more while you have the chance. Now we come to another example of a sub-rational reaction which can wisely be overruled.

There are in our emotional-instinctual nature two deep motivations, which are often called the Fight-or-Flight instincts. When anything threatens us or hurts us, we are prompted to react according to these instincts. Whether we feel inclined to fight back at the cause of the trouble or to run away from it, will depend upon a number of factors; but as a beginning, no matter which it is to be, the nerves become extra alert and the muscles tense up ready to take action.

Supposing the threat is something which calls for neither fight nor flight, like so many in civilized living? Then you can end up with a "tension headache", which does not help you cope with anything. Or supposing you have a physical pain, such as those we have been discussing? Muscular tension will, in most cases, do no good at all. In fact it can do harm, for tense muscles restrict the circulation of the blood which should go to the hurting part; and some of the uses of the circulation are to carry away impurities, to reduce inflammation, to nourish nerves and tissues.

Here, therefore, you will do well to override the action of your emotional-instinctual nature, and with your rational mind to guide your body through a progressive relaxation. But additionally, you should give your Deep Mind some good work to do. You can convey to it, by means of Creative Visualization, a helpful image to activate—those cool, healing fingers for instance—and, using this image, it can bring about results your rational mind would be quite unable to produce by its own abilities.

Fresh air for many people these days is where they find it. If you live within reach of open country or seashore, that's the best; but a session of Rhythmic Breathing indoors among your oxygen friends (green plants which take in the carbon dioxide you breathe *out,* and give out oxygen for you to breathe *in*) is better for your lungs and your blood than jogging alongside a freeway laden with exhaust fumes.

Creative Visualization has a very real and traditional part to play in Rhythmic Breathing, particularly in a session of breathing performed expressly for the good of your health.

Air, particularly gently-moving, sunlit air of a con-genial temperature, is a good mixture. We want plenty of oxygen, but not the undiluted article; while the presence of a small percentage of carbon dioxide, and enough water vapor to be easy on our lungs, keeps our breathing within the range of normality. Air has other ingedients too, and its composition can in fact vary quite a fair amount and still fulfill the purposes for which air is needed by our bodies. Once you have settled to your Rhythmic Breathing in the best air you can find, therefore, all you need think about is the main process which is happening: when air reaches your lungs the oxygen in it is taken over by your blood, which then carries it through your body for the nourishment and renewal of every tissue; the blood continually receiving in exchange for its supply of oxygen the carbonic acid which the tissues discard, and, having circulated back to the lungs, cleansing itself by shedding carbon dioxide into the air which you exhale.

That is a simplification, but what you need here is *a clear mental picture,* not a complicated study in physiology.

Easily, while you breathe—and particularly while you do Rhythmic Breathing—you can imagine this sustaining and health-renewing process going on; as you breathe in, "seeing" the oxygen being carried swiftly by your blood to every part of your body, and as you breathe out "seeing" your blood carrying impurities back to your lungs and there expelling them.

But you can go beyond the merely physical level. You can do more for yourself than that.

Visualize the Light of your Higher Self surrounding you, bright and life-giving.

As you breathe in, "feel" that Light—radiant, warm, bearing joy and comfort—being inhaled by you along with the air, being taken into your lungs, into your blood, shining in your heart and all through your body as it spreads peace, strength and blessing. ("Send" it, by willing and imagining it, particularly into any region of your body which needs help. Practice sending increased circulation and warmth to cold hands and feet by this means, for example.)

When you breathe out, along with the carbon dioxide and other material impurities "feel" departing also any tiredness, negative thoughts, doubts or fears which may have troubled you. On the next in-breath, *along with the oxygen-laden air draw into yourself again joy, peace, strength and blessing, all borne on radiant spiritual Light.*

This practice, you will realize, is *not* "all imagination". Your Higher Self really is there all the time, and the awareness of its presence is all Light and Love: unconquerable Light and Love. To receive its blessings you have only to be aware, to open yourself to it in confidence, to be willing to experience that strength and joy. The practice of Rhythmic Breathing gives you an opportunity to do this.

In this way, the air you are breathing is not only an effective physical good; it becomes *a powerful symbol* to bring you a greater spiritual good. People have always used material things in this way, to carry the real spiritual power of what the things physically do or stand for: salt used as a spiritual antiseptic, a ring or a cord to make a spiritual union, a knife or a sword to make division, water for spiritual washing and a new beginning. The Deep Mind understands and accepts this sign-language, and receives the spiritual reality along with the sign. So here, along with the physical purifying, renewing and life-giving power of the air you breathe, you can send to every part of your inner being—*in a form your Deep Mind will know and accept*—the blessing, the love and the life of your **Higher Self.**

Exercise is another essential key to maintaining and improving health. Practically everyone needs exercise of one sort or another; and with all exercises, however elaborate or simple, gentle or strenuous, there is scope for improved performance and increased benefit through the use of Creative Visualization.

For every exercise you include in your routine, you ought in any case to know exactly what muscles it affects and what you can expect from it. Take one of your exercises and, *before doing it,* reflect quietly on what it does and what it is for. Next, visualize yourself doing this exercise accurately and perfectly. If you like, go in this way through several exercises which are familiar to you. *Then do them:* in front of a large mirror if possible, or, while doing them, renew your visualization of yourself in action. Your enjoyment, your performance and the good you gain from these exercises should be noticeably improved.

If you swim, run, play tennis or football, whatever physical recreation may be yours, sit quietly sometimes and in your imgination go through the motions: not idly, but with care. Physical "warming-up" is a good thing, so is this imaginative "warming-up"; for it involves the other half of body-mind co-ordination. You can take it further, visualize yourself going through the actions of a winning performance. This will not take the place of physical practice, but it can supplement it very effectively.

And supposing you find you have an opponent who also does Creative Visualization? Then it will be a great experience for both of you, for you'll both be at the top of your form!

STAY IN TOUCH

On the following pages you will find listed, with their current prices, some of the books and tapes now available on related subjects. Your book dealer stocks most of these, and will stock new titles in the Llewellyn series as they become available. We urge your patronage.

However, to obtain our full catalog, to keep informed of new titles as they are released and to benefit from informative articles and helpful news, you are invited to write for our bi-monthly news magazine/catalog. A sample copy is free, and it will continue coming to you at no cost as long as you are an active mail customer. Or you may keep it coming for a full year with a donation of just $2.00 in U.S.A. ($7.00 for Canada & Mexico, $20.00 overseas, first class mail). Many bookstores also have *The Llewellyn New Times* available to their customers. Ask for it.

Stay in touch! In *The Llewellyn New Times'* pages you will find news and reviews of new books, tapes and services, announcements of meetings and seminars, articles helpful to our readers, news of authors, advertising of products and services, special money-making opportunities, and much more.

The Llewellyn New Times
P.O. Box 64383-183, St. Paul, MN 55164-0383, U.S.A.

•   •   •

TO ORDER BOOKS AND TAPES

If your book dealer does not have the books and tapes described on the following pages readily available, you may order them direct from the publisher by sending full price in U.S. funds, plus $1.00 for handling and 50¢ each book or item for postage within the United States; outside USA surface mail add $1.00 extra per item. Outside USA air mail add $7.00 per item.

FOR GROUP STUDY AND PURCHASE

Because there is a great deal of interest in group discussion and study of the subject matter of this book, we feel that we should encourage the adoption and use of this particular book by such groups by offering a special "quantity" price to group leaders or agents".

Our Special Quality Price for a minimum order of five copies of THE LLEWELLYN PRACTICAL GUIDE TO CREATIVE VISUALIZATION is $23.85 Cash-With-Order. This price includes postage and handling within the United States. Minnesota residents must add 6% sales tax. For additional quantities, please order in multiples of five. For Canadian and foreign orders, add postage and handling charges as above. Credit Card (VISA, MasterCard, American Express, Diners' Club) Orders are accepted. Charge Card Orders only may be phoned free ($15.00 minimum order) within the U.S.A. by dialing 1-800-THE MOON (in Canada call: 1-800-FOR-SELF). Customer Service calls dial 1-612-291-1970 and ask for "Kae." Mail Orders to:

LLEWELLYN PUBLICATIONS
P.O. Box 64383-183 / St. Paul, MN 55164-0383, U.S.A.

THE LLEWELLYN DEEP MIND TAPE FOR CREATIVE VISUALIZATION

The Deep Mind Creative Visualization Tape is designed to help you attain your objectives by means of the most powerful single technique existing: Creative Visualization. You should use it to accompany your work with the *Llewellyn Practical Guide to Creative Visualization.*

The powers needed to make your dreams come true are within you *now.* You don't need to wait until you have developed or evolved to a high level before you can use those powers effectively. They are part of the natural heritage of every living being. We humans have to learn to use consciously abilities which other creatures exercise instinctively. But when we have learned them we can exercise those abilities with a unique force and with an unlimited range of application.

Creative Visualization is a truly creative and immensely effective procedure which, when you understand how to use and direct it, places a vast natural force at the disposal of your will and your imagination. This force truly is unlimited: the only limits it can ever have, for you, are the limits of what you desire and the limits of what you can use and enjoy. And you can expand those boundaries as you proceed.

The Deep Mind Creative Visualization Tape will guide you in the use of Creative Visualization to gain specific objectives. This present tape is designed to help you gain such objectives as material possessions, or the development of a talent, or for success on some specially important occasion. When you have gained your present objective, you can use this tape again whenever you feel like it, to reinforce your success, to gain other objectives, and to enter more deeply, with practice, into Creative Visualization.

The Llewellyn Practical Guide to Creative Visualization is the basic text, teaching you all the techniques you need for performing Creative Visualization effectively, and making clear also the reasons for everything you should do. You should read that helpful and inspiring book right through at least once, thoughtfully and carefully, before beginning to make practical use of this tape. So also with any other Deep Mind Creative Visualization Tapes you may choose for special purposes; in all cases you should read this *Practical Guide* through from time to time, to ensure you are keeping close to all of its vital counsels and its positive affirmations.

0-87542-169-5 $9.95

Note: If you have the book, THE LLEWELLYN PRACTICAL GUIDE TO CREATIVE VISUALIZATION, you may order this DEEP MIND TAPE by sending full price, plus $1.50 postage & handling ($7.00 overseas airmail). Or, you can order both Book AND Tape for a special price of just $15.00 Postpaid in U.S.A. ($25.00 overseas airmail).

THE LLEWELLYN PRACTICAL GUIDES
by Melita Denning & Osborne Phillips

THE LLEWELLYN PRACTICAL GUIDE TO ASTRAL PROJECTION.
Yes, your consciousness can be sent forth, out-of-the-body, with full
awareness and return with full memory. You can travel through time and
space, converse with non-physical entities, obtain knowledge by non-
material means, and experience higher dimensions.

> **Is there life-after-death? Are we forever shackled by Time & Space?
> The ability to go forth by means of the Astral Body, or Body of
> Light, gives the personal assurance of consciousness (and life)
> beyond the limitations of the physical body. No other answer to
> these ageless questions is as meaningful as experienced reality.**

The reader is led through the essential stages for the inner growth and
development that will culminate in fully conscious projection and return.
Not only are the requisite practices set forth in step-by-step procedures,
augmented with photographs and puts-you-in-the-picture" visualization aids, but the vital reasons for undertaking them are clearly explained.
Beyond this, the great benefits from the various practices themselves are
demonstrated in renewed physical and emotional health, mental discipline, spiritual attainment, and the development of extra faculties".

Guidance is also given to the Astral World itself: what to expect, what can
be done—including the ecstatic experience of Astral Sex between two
people who project together into this higher world where true union is
consumated free of the barriers of physical bodies.

0-87542-181-4, 239 pages, 5¼ x 8, softcover   **$7.95**

THE LLEWELLYN DEEP MIND TAPE FOR ASTRAL PROJECTION.
This is a tool so powerful that it is offered only for use in conjunction with
the above book. The authors of this book are adepts fully experienced in
all levels of psychic development and training, and have designed this
90-minute cassette tape to guide the student through full relaxation and
all the preparations for projection, and then—with the added dimension
of the authors personally produced electronic synthesizer patterns of
sound and music—they program the Deep Mind through the stages of
awakening, and projection of, the astral Body of Light. And then the
programming guides your safe return to normal consciousness with
memory—enabling you to bridge the worlds of Body, Mind and Spirit.

> **The Deep Mind Tape is a powerful new technique combining
> guided Mind Programming with specially created sound and
> music to evoke deep level response in the psyche and its psychic
> centres for controlled development, and induction of the OUT-
> OF-BODY EXPERIENCE.**

3-87542-201, 90-minute cassette tape.   **$9.95**

Note: If you have the book, THE LLEWELLYN PRACTICAL GUIDE TO ASTRAL PROJECTION, you may order
this DEEP MIND TAPE by sending full price, plus $1.50 postage & handling ($7.00 overseas airmail). Or,
you can order both Book AND Tape for a special price of just $15.00 Postpaid in U.S.A. ($25.00 overseas
airmail).

THE LLEWELLYN PRACTICAL GUIDE TO THE MAGICK OF THE TAROT.
How to Read, And Shape, Your Future.

"To gain understanding, *and control*, of Your Life,"—Can anything be more important? To gain insight into the circumstances of your life—the inner causes, the karmic needs, the hidden factors at work—and then to have the power to change your life in order to fulfill your real desires and True Will: that's what the techniques taught in this book can do.

Discover the Shadows cast ahead by Coming Events.

Yes, this is possible, because it is your DEEP MIND—that part of your psyche, normally beyond your conscious awareness, which is in touch with the World Soul and with your own Higher (and Divine) Self—that perceives the *astral shadows* of coming events and can communicate them to you through the symbols and images of the ancient and mysterious Tarot Cards.

This book teaches you both how to read the Tarot Cards: seeing the likely outcome of the present trends and the hidden forces now at work shaping tomorrow's circumstances, and then—as never before presented to the public—how you can expand this same system to bring these causal forces under your conscious control.

> The MAGICK of the Tarot mobilizes the powerful inner resources of psyche and soul (the source of all Magick, all seemingly miraculous powers) by means of meditation, ritual, drama, dance for the attainment of your goals, including your spiritual growth.

0-87542-198-9, 252 pages, 5¼ x 8, illust., softcover. $7.95

THE LLEWELLYN PRACTICAL GUIDE TO PSYCHIC SELF-DEFENSE AND WELL-BEING. Psychic Well-Being and Psychic Self-Defense are two sides of the same coin—just as physical health and resistance to disease are:

> **FACT: Each person (and every living thing) is surrounded by an electro-magnetic Force Field, or AURA, that can provide the means to Psychic Self-Defense and to dynamic Well-Being.**

This book explores the world of very real "psychic warfare" that we all are victims of:

> **FACT: Every person in our modern world is subjected, constantly, to psychic stress and psychological bombardment: advertising and sales promotions that play upon primitive emotions, political and religious appeals that work on feelings of insecurity and guilt, noise, threats of violence and war, news of crime and disaster, etc.**

This book shows the nature of genuine psychic attacks—ranging from actual acts of black magic to bitter jealousy and hate—and the reality of psychic stress, the structure of the psyche and its inter-relationship with the physical body. It shows how each person must develop his weakened aura into a powerful defense-shield—thereby gaining both physical protection and energetic well-being that can extend to protection from physical violence, accidents . . . even ill-health.

> **FACT: This book can change your life! Your developed aura brings you strength, confidence, poise . . . the dynamics for success, and for communion with your Spiritual Source.**

This book gives exact instructions for the fortification of the aura, specific techniques for protection, and the Rite of the First Kathisma using the PSALMS to invoke Divine Blessing. Illustrated with "puts-you-into-the-picture" drawings, and includes powerful techniques not only for your personal use but for group use.

0-87542-190-3, 277 pages, 5¼ x 8, softcover. $7.95

THE LLEWELLYN PRACTICAL GUIDE TO THE DEVELOPMENT OF PSYCHIC POWERS. You may not realize it, but . . . you already have the ability to use ESP, Astral Vision and Clairvoyance, Divination, Dowsing, Prophecy, Communications with Spirits, Mental Telepathy, etc. WE ALL HAVE THESE POWERS! It's simply a matter of knowing what to do, and then to exercise (as with any talent) and develop them.

Written by two of the most knowledgeable experts in the world of Magick today, this book is a complete course—teaching you, step-by-step, how to develop these powers that actually have been yours since birth. Using the techniques they teach, you will soon be able to move objects at a distance, see into the future, know the thoughts and feelings of another person, find lost objects, locate water and even people using your own no-longer latent talents.

Psychic powers are as much a natural ability as any other talent. You'll learn to play with those new skills, work with groups of friends to accomplish things you never would have believed possible before reading this book. The text shows you how to make the equipment you can use, the exercises you can do—many of them at any time, anywhere—and how to use your abilities to change your life and the lives of those close to you. Many of the exercises are presented in forms that can be adapted as games for pleasure and fun, as well as development. Illustrated throughout.
ISBN: 0-87542-191-1, 244 pages, 5¼ x 8, soft cover. $7.95

CUNNINGHAM'S ENCYCLOPEDIA OF MAGICAL HERBS
by Scott Cunningham

This is an expansion on the material presented in his first Llewellyn book, *Magical Herbalism*. This is not just another herbal for medicinal uses of herbs; this is the most comprehensive source of herbal data for magical uses. Each of the over 400 herbs are illustrated and the magical properties, planetary rulerships, genders, deities, folk and latin names are given. There is a large annotated bibliography, a list of mail order suppliers, a folk name cross reference, and all the herbs are fully indexed. No other book like it exists. Find out what herbs to use for luck, love, success, money, divination, astral projection and much more. Fun, interesting and fully illustrated with unusual woodcuts from old herbals.

0-87542-122-9, 6 x 9, 350 pp., illustrated, softcover. $12.95

EARTH POWER: TECHNIQUES OF NATURAL MAGIC
by Scott Cunningham

Magick is the art of working with the forces of Nature to bring about necessary, and desired, changes. The forces of Nature—expressed through Earth, Air, Fire and Water—are our "spiritual ancestors" who paved the way for our emergence from the pre-historic seas of creation. Attuning to, and working with these energies in magick not only lends you the power to affect changes in your life, it also allows you to sense your own place in the larger scheme of Nature. Using the "Old Ways" enables you to live a better life, and to deepen your understanding of the world about you. The tools and powers of magick are around you, waiting to be grasped and utilized. This book gives you the means to put Magick into your life, shows you how to make and use the tools, and gives you spells for every purpose.
0-87542-121-0, 250 pages, illust., soft cover. $6.95

PRACTICAL CANDLEBURNING RITUALS
by Raymond Buckland, Ph. D.

Another book in Llewellyn's Practical Magick series. Magick is a way in which to apply the full range of your hidden psychic powers to the problems we all face in daily life. We know that normally we use only 5% of our total powers—Magick taps powers from deep inside our psyche where we are in contact with the Universe's limitless resources.

Magick need not be complex—it can be as simple as using a few candles to focus your mind, a simple ritual to give direction to your desire, a few words to give expression to your wish.

This book shows you how easy it can be. Here is Magick for fun, Magick as a Craft, Magick for Success, Love, Luck, Money, Marriage, Healing; Magick to stop slander, to learn truth, to heal an unhappy marriage, to overcome a bad habit, to break up a love affair, etc.

Magick—with nothing fancier than ordinary candles, and the 28 rituals in this book (given in both Christian and Old Religion versions)—can transform your life.
ISBN: 0-87542-048-06, 189 pg., 5¼ x 8, Illus., softbound. **$5.95**

MAGICAL HERBALISM—The Secret Craft of the Wise
by Scott Cunningham

In Magical Herbalism, certain plants are prized for the special range of energies—the vibrations, or powers—they possess. Magical Herbalism unites the powers of plants and man to produce, and direct, change in accord with human will and desire. This is the Magic of amulets and charms, sachets and herbal pillows, incenses and scented oils, simples and infusions and annointments. It's Magic as old as our knowledge of plants, an art that anyone can learn and practice, and once again enjoy as we look to the Earth to re-discover our roots and make inner connections with the world of Nature.

This is Magic that is beautiful and natural—a Craft of Hand and Mind merged with the Power and Glory of Nature: a special kind that does not use the medicinal powers of herbs, but rather the subtle vibrations and scents that touch the psychic centers and stir the astral field in which we live to work at the causal level behind the material world.

This is the Magic of Enchantment . . . of word and gesture to shape the images of mind and channel the energies of the herbs. It is a Magic for *everyone*—for the herbs are easily and readily obtained, the tools are familiar or easily made, and the technology that of home and garden.

This book includes step-by-step guidance to the preparation of herbs and to their compounding in incesnse and oils, sachets and amulets, simples and infusions, with simple rituals and spells for every purpose.
ISBN: 0-87542-120-2, 243 pgs., 5¼ x 8, illustrated, soft cover. **$7.95**

MAGICAL RITES FROM THE CRYSTAL WELL
by Ed Fitch
In nature, and in the Earth, we look and find beauty. Within ourselves we find a well from which we may draw truth and knowledge. And when we draw from this well, we rediscover that we are all children of the Earth.
The simple rites in this book are presented to you as a means of finding your own way back to nature; for discovering and experiencing the beauty and the magic of unity with the source.
These are the celebrations of the seasons: at the same time they are rites by which we attune ourselves to the flow of the force—the energy of life. These are rites of passage by which we celebrate the major transitions we all experience in life.

Here are the Old Ways, but they are also the Ways for Today.

0-87542-230-6, 147 pages, 7 x 10, illust.   **$9.95**

PRACTICAL COLOR MAGICK by Raymond Buckland
The world is a rainbow of color, a symphony of vibration. We have left the Newtonian idea of the world as being made of large mechanical units, and now know it as a strange chaos of vibrations ordered by our senses, but, our senses are limited and designed by Nature to give us access to only those vibratory emanations we need for survival.

But, we live far from the natural world now. And the colors which filled our habitats when we were natural creatures have given way to grey and black and synthetic colors of limited wave lengths determined not by our physiological needs but by economic constraints.

Raymond Buckland, author of the world-famous PRACTICAL CANDLE BURNING RITUALS has produced a fascinating and useful new book, PRACTICAL GUIDE FOR COLOR MAGICKwhich shows you how to reintroduce color into your life to benefit your physical, mental and spiritual well-being!
- Learn the secret meanings of color.
- Use color to change the energy centers of your body.
- Heal yourself and others through light radiation.
- Discover the hidden aspects of your personality through color.

PRACTICAL COLOR MAGICK will teach all the powers of light and more! You'll learn new forms of expression of your inner-most self, new ways of relating to others with the secret languages of light and color. Put true color back into your life with the rich spectrum of ideas and practical magical formulas from PRACTICAL COLOR MAGICK!

0-87542-047-8, 200 pp., illustrated   **$5.95**

THE LLEWELLYN MYSTERY RELIGION SERIES

VOUDOUN FIRE: THE LIVING REALITY OF MYSTICAL RELIGION.
by Melita Denning & Osborne Phillips, photography by Gloria Rudolph.
OBJECTIVE PROOF OF SPIRITUAL REALITY. Here are spectacular full color photographs of actual psychic phenomena filmed during Voodoo rituals in Haiti . . . giving objective proof of powers and forces normally invisible, and of the Power and the Glory that is part of all valid religious, and magical, experience.

"This is a book of revelation!

"In it, the objective reality of the Loa—Haitian Gods—and of the paranormal phenomena of mystical religion is demonstrated.

"The fact that this is demonstrated through a level of consciousness not ordinarily experienced confirms the ancient teachings that it is we—not the Gods—who must open the way. And when we do, the Gods respond.

"This book restores religious phenomena to us, and at the same time reveals the likelihood that anyone of European descent can be sure that at least some of his ancestors followed religions very similar to Voudoun. Thus we see that such a powerful mystical religion with the personal experience of paranormal phenomena is our rightful heritage!

"Indeed—all Gods are One God—and the intimate and direct contact between Man and divinity, the continued presence of invisible powers, and the revelation needed by modern man if we are to save ourselves from total alienation from the Natural World that is our proper home.

"Yes, these photographs require the recognition of other dimensions to reality. But we are living in an Age when we see that all men are—as seen from another dimension—One Man, and that all life is but One Life. The plurality of the Gods is likewise a matter of dimension, but it is from this dimension that we must reach up to make contact with Divinity. It is for us to make a channel for the Power to manifest. And of the Christian churches, it is the Catholic Power, that resembles Voudoun sufficiently so that many of the Haitian Gods, as well as those of Santeria and other Spiritist religions, can be seen as saints in a different dress.

"Fire has always been associated with the Gods, and in these photographs, we see why: we see the "astral light" as streamers of Cosmic Fire. Perhaps, too, we can gain an understanding of Fire as a "gift of the Gods", for it is contact with this Cosmic Fire that seems to bring about the paranormal phenomena, the "going invisible", for example, of the mystical religions.

"When we restore the paranormal to religions, and when we see the role of religious worship as the opening of channels between Man and Divinity, then we also see the joyous relationship between Man and Nature, Man and man, and Man and the Spiritual Worlds. And we learn that all religions are One Religion, and in this we also find the necessity for the many ways through which men reach the Gods and relate to Divine Power."

(from the introduction, by Carl Llewellyn Weschcke, Publisher)

In this book, you see for yourself the ASTRAL FIRE that accompanies genuine ritual; you see the living presence of the LOA (the Haitian God-forces) as they are invoked; you witness the visible possession of the devotee by a spiritual entity, and the ecstasy upon her face. The text gives a concise history of Voudoun, tracing not only its African but AmerIndian origins and its beginnings back into ancient Egypt. Parallels with Christianity and with pre-Christian European religions are demonstrated, and the distorted myths which represent Voodoo as evil are shown for what they are. The religion itself is analyzed, its dances, chants, musical and magical instruments, its gods and rituals described. Voudoun is made to come alive for the reader and its music is presented in words and score set to disco beat for personal experience.

0-87542-186-5, 182 pages, 8½ x 11, 39 full page color plates, and nearly 100 black and white photographs and drawings.
Softbound. $9.95

FANTASY JOURNEYS
Narrated Quests of the Mind and Spirit by Ed Fitch

In this series of guided imagery sessions, Ed Fitch takes you on inner journeys to some very real realms of Magick where your Mind and Spirit explore and learn, create and enjoy, and come back enriched.

These tapes are based on Ed's extensive knowledge and years of practice and teaching. They combine aspects of Jungian Psychology, Qabalah and Magick, and the Pagan World Views into a composite of high technological application to fulfill your need for guidance into new worlds of consciousness.

TAPE I
SIDE 1: THE ARMOR OF LIGHT. You will be led on an adventure during which you will find your personal suit of armor, constructed with your own hands out of resources from the inner world. Here is an adventure with real meaning in your explorations of other dimensions.

0SIDE 2: AUDIENCE WITH THE SEA QUEEN. Moon Magick, Ocean Magick, the Lady of the Skies, the Lady of the Ocean Depths. Meet Her, explore Her realm and gain the powers that contact with this Archetype alone can give.

TAPE II
SIDE 1: JOURNEY TO THE LAND OF YESOD. Within the Qabalah's Tree of Life there is a strange world ruled by the Moon. It is an Astral World with its own laws and strange powers you can learn to wield as you adventure through it with Ed's guidance.

SIDE 2: DRAGON RIDE. The Dragon is an age-old symbol of the active Female principle: creation embodied in a horrific and strange beast. On this quest, you will seach out the dragon, understand it and harness its energies . . . or will it do the same to you, instead?

TAPE III
SIDE 1: VISIT TO THE ELVISH HILLS. The true Lords of the Night are the Elves and fairies. Meet them, understand them, and know their power. You will be rewarded, and you will never be quite the same again.

SIDE 2: THRONE OF THE GOLDEN AGES. The Tree is huge and powerful, old and venerable . . . its roots sunk deep into being. Climb the great Tree and discover the throne of a Demigod. Take Its place, and know Its power yourself.

TAPE IV
SIDE 1: BUILDING AN ASTRAL TEMPLE. From materials of the astral world: astral wood, stone, air and fire, you build a temple of the soul. Your design, Your power, Your Symbols of Being are all incorporated into this mighty structure, built and filled with the power of your magick.

SIDE2: VISIT TO THE CAVE OF APHRODITE. Journey to the beginning of Creation, walk with the spirits of Aphrodite's world of beauty and power. Here is the inner home of the True Pagan.

Each tape cassette is 60 minutes in length, priced at $9.95, or $32.00 for the set of four. To order direct, please add $1.00 handling per order, and .50 per tape for postage.

ETERNAL DANCE by LaVedi Laffery & Bud Hollowell

THERE IS NO LIFE AFTER DEATH—THERE IS NO DEATH!

The Spirit is the essence of each individual and it cannot be destroyed. The body and its worldly identity are like suits of clothes you exchange as your True Self moves through one manifestation to another. Explore the incredible world of reincarnation and the implications of its reality in Lafferty and Hollowell's **ETERNAL DANCE**, an exciting new book from Llewellyn Publications.
ISBN: 0-87542-436-8, 512 pp., illustrated.   **$9.95**

ALSO AVAILABLE

Lafferty and Hollowell have developed a series of tapes which are designed to take you into your past lives and allow you to experience those events which have shaped your present personality and existence:

No. 1 HOW PAST LIVES EFFECT THE PRESENT. How Karma works and what it means in your present.

No. 2 HOW TO USE THE POWERS OF HYPNOSIS. Introduction to the basics of self-hypnosis, essential to Past Life exploration.

No. 3 JOURNEY INTO THE PAST WITH A LOVED ONE. Discover the past links between you and those close to you in the present life.

No. 4 FINDING SOLUTIONS TO PRESENT LIFE PROBLEMS. Present problems begin in past situations. Discover the means for important breakthroughs to solutions.

No. 5 DISCOVER HIDDEN TALENTS, ABILITIES AND KNOWLEDGE. Tap the resources from earlier lives. Tapes 3, 4, and 5 have on side two the very effective **BODY OF LIGHT INDUCTION** exercise, designed to help you find peace and a loving center with yourself.

Each tape is $9.95. A set of all five tapes is available for $39.95. You save over $9.00!

CRYSTAL POWER
by Michael G. Smith

This is an amazing book, for what it claims to present—with complete instructions and diagrams so that YOU can work them yourself—is the master technology of ancient Atlantis: psionic (mind-controlled and life-energized machines) devices made from common quartz crystals!

These Crystal Devices seem to work only with the disciplined mind power of a human operator, yet their very construction seems to start a process of growth and development, a new evolutionary step in the human psyche that bridges mind and matter.

Does this "re-discovery" mean that we are living, now, in The New Atlantis? Have these Power Tools been re-invented to meet the needs of this prophetic time? Are Psionic Machines the culminating Power To The People to free us from economic dependence on fossil fuels and smokestack industry?

This book answers "yes" to all these questions, and asks you to simply build these devices and put them to work to help bring it all about.
0-87542-725-1, illust., soft   **$9.95**

THE LLEWELLYN ANNUALS

Llewellyn's MOON SIGN BOOK: approximately 400 pages of valuable information on gardening, fishing, weather, stock market forecasts, personal horoscopes, good planting dates, and general instructions for finding the best date to do just about anything! Articles by prominent forecasters and writers in the fields of gardening, astrology, politics, economics and cycles. This special almanac, different from any other, has been published annually since 1906. It's fun, informative and has been a great help to millions in their daily planning.

State year $3.95

Llewellyn's SUN SIGN BOOK: Your personal horoscope for the entire year! All 12 signs are included in one handy book. Also included are political and economic forecasts, special feature articles, and lucky dates for each sign. Monthly horoscopes by a prominent radio and TV astrologer for your personal Sun Sign. Articles on a variety of subjects written by well-known astrologers from around the country. Much more than just a horoscope guide! Entertaining and fun the year round.

State year $3.95

Llewellyn's DAILY PLANETARY GUIDE and ASTROLOGER'S DATE-BOOK: Includes all of the major daily aspects plus their exact times in Eastern and Pacific time zones, lunar phases, signs and voids plus their times, planetary motion, a monthly ephemeris, sunrise and sunset tables, special articles on the planets, signs, aspects, a business guide, planetary hours, rulerships, and much more. Large 5¼ × 8 format for more writing space, spiral bound to lay flat, address and phone listings, time zone conversion chart and blank horoscope chart.

State year $6.95

Llewellyn's ASTROLOGICAL CALENDAR: Large wall calendar of 52 pages. Beautiful full color cover and color inside. Includes special feature articles by famous astrologers, introductory information on astrology, Lunar Gardening Guide, celestial phenomena for the year, a blank horoscope chart for your own chart data, and monthly date pages which include aspects, lunar information, planetary motion, ephemeris, personal forecasts, lucky dates, planting and fishing dates, and more. 10 x 13 size. Set in Central time, with conversion table for other time zones worldwide.

State year $6.95

MAGICAL STATES OF CONSCIOUSNESS
by Melita Denning and Osborne Phillips

Magical States of Consciousness are dimensions of the Human Psyche giving us access to the knowledge and powers of the Great Archetypes.

These dimensions are attained as we travel the Paths of the Qabalah's Tree of Life—that "blueprint" to the structure of the Lesser Universe of the Human Psyche and to the Greater Universe in which we have our being.

Published here for the first time are not only the complete texts for these inward journeys to the Deep Unconscious Mind, but complete guidance to their application in Spiritual Growth and Initiation, Psychological Integration and "Soul Sculpture" (the secret technique by which we may shape our own character).

Here, too, are *Magical Mandalas* for each of the PathWorkings that serve as "doorways" to altered states of consciousness when used with the Path-Working narrations, and *Magical Images* of the Sephirothic Archetypes as used in invoking those powerful forces.

0-87542-194-6, 420 pages, Illust.,soft. **$12.95**

THE LLEWELLYN INNER GUIDE TAPES

Because Path-working has so many benefits to the Listener/Participant, we are making the texts of each of the Path-workings in *Magical States of Consciousness* available on high-quality cassette tapes.

Each tape is accompanied by a booklet of necessary instructions, with the appropriate Magical Mandala for the path being worked.
45 min. to each side, $12.95 each.

32nd Path: Governing Intelligence, 3L151 Development intuition, enhance astral projection, and creative visualization.

31st Path: Unresting Intelligence
30th Path: Collating Intelligence 3L152, 31st Path develops courage, enhances past life recall, arouses Kundalini, frees you from emotional conditioning. 30th Path enhances healing powers, develops discipline, assist in visualization operations.

29th Path: The Bodily Intelligence
28th Path: The Perfecting Intelligence 3L153, 29th Path spreads harmony, heals family disputes, assists with helping animals, increases prosperity, enhances scrying. 28th Path disciplines the mind, helps in astrological analysis, planning career.

27th Path: Awakening Intelligence, 3L154, Courage to face fears, skill in avoiding quarrels, banishing in magical rites, increases debating skills, love.

26th Path, Part I: The Renewing Intelligence 24th Path, Part I: Image-making Intelligence 3L155.

(All of the following are 60 minute tapes, $9.95)

26th Path, Part 2, 3L157 24th Path, Part 2, 3L158
26th Path gives access to inner powers and outer control over tendency to domineer. Used for exorcism, rites of protection for home. Promotes generosity and tolerance. 24th Path assuages grief, resolves inner conflicts. Used for Sex Magick, helps in understanding adolescents,

25th Path: Critical Intelligence, 3L156 Strengthens the bonds with the Higher Self, promotes spiritual progress, develops self-confidence, assists in calling up God Forms, astral projection, invoking HGA. Protection while traveling.

THE INNER WORLD OF FITNESS
Melita Denning

Because the artificialities and the daily hassles of routine living tend to turn our attention from the real values, *The Inner World of Fitness* leads us back by means of those natural factors in life which remain to us: air, water, sunlight, the food we eat, the world of nature, meditation, sexual love and the power of our own wishes—so that through these things we can re-link ourselves in awareness to the great non-material forces of life and of being which underlie them.

The unity and interaction of inner and outer, keeping body and psyche open to the great currents of life and of the natural forces, is seen as the essential secret of *youthfulness* and hence of radiant fitness. Regardless of our physical age, so long as we are within the flow of these great currents, we have the vital quality of youthfulness: but if we begin to close off or turn away from those contacts, in the same measure we begin to lose youthfulness.

0-87542-165-2, 240 pgs., 5¼ x 8, softcover. $7.95